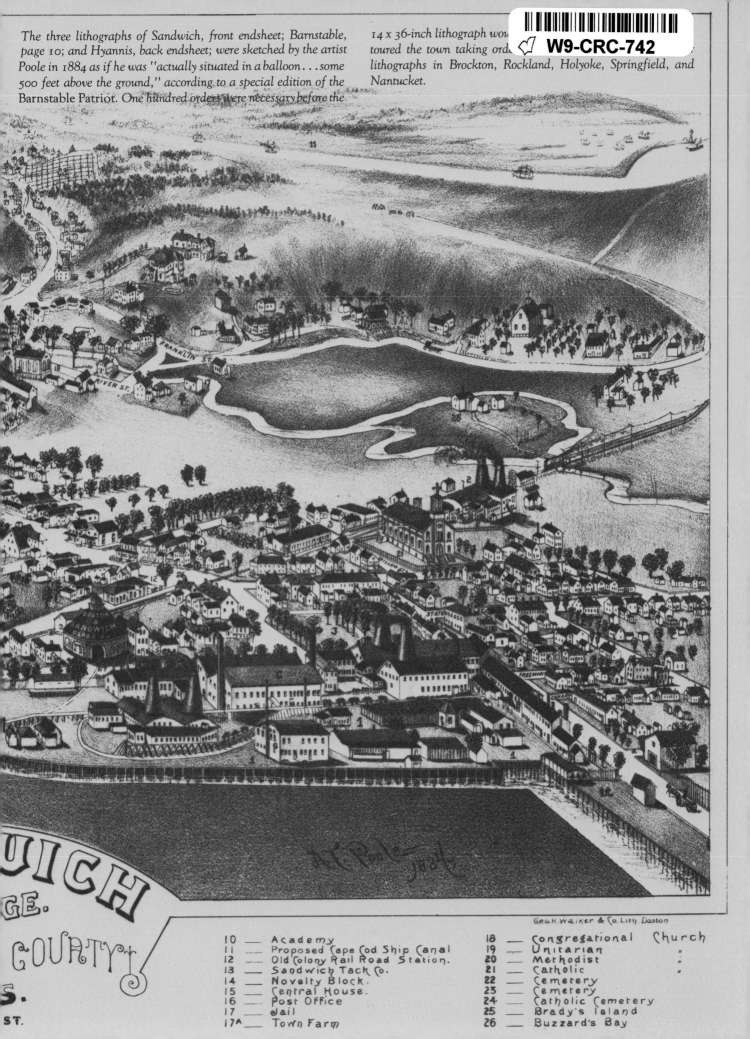

The three lithographs of Sandwich, front endsheet; Barnstable, page 10; and Hyannis, back endsheet; were sketched by the artist Poole in 1884 as if he was "actually situated in a balloon...some 500 feet above the ground," according to a special edition of the Barnstable Patriot. One hundred orders were necessary before the 14 x 36-inch lithograph would [be printed?]. [He?] toured the town taking ord[ers?] ... lithographs in Brockton, Rockland, Holyoke, Springfield, and Nantucket.

Geo.H.Walker & Co. Lith. Boston

10 — Academy	18 — Congregational Church
11 — Proposed Cape Cod Ship Canal	19 — Unitarian
12 — Old Colony Rail Road Station.	20 — Methodist
13 — Sandwich Tack Co.	21 — Catholic
14 — Novelty Block.	22 — Cemetery
15 — Central House.	23 — Cemetery
16 — Post Office	24 — Catholic Cemetery
17 — Jail	25 — Brady's Island
17A — Town Farm	26 — Buzzard's Bay

Sentry Bank is pleased
to make possible this
limited edition of
Cape Cod: a Pictorial History.
This carefully documented and
beautifully designed volume
will prove a valuable addition
to your library and a
collector's item as the years pass.

In appreciation of the
continuing trust placed in us
by the people of our community,
we dedicate this book
to the citizens of Cape Cod
—past, present and future.

Joseph W. Higgins

Joseph W. Higgins
President
Sentry Cooperative Bank

Cape Cod
a pictorial history

by **Marion Vuilleumier**
design by **Jamie Backus Raynor**
Donning Company/Publishers
Norfolk/Virginia Beach

Library of Congress Cataloging in
Publication Data:

Vuilleumier, Marion.
  Cape Cod, a pictorial history.

  Bigliography: p.
  Includes index.
  1. Cape Cod (Mass.)—History—Pictorial
works.
  2. Cape Cod (Mass.)—Description and
travel—Views. I. Title.
F72.C3V79 1982   974.4'92 82-9556
ISBN 0-89865-263-4

Printed in the United States of America

Contents

Foreword 7
Preface 9
Acknowledgements 11
The Wampanoags
    (thru-1620) 13
The Pilgrims
    (1620-1636) 21
An Arm of the Old Colony
    (1637-1692) 33
Massachusetts vs.the Crown
    (1693-1819) 55
Prosperity
    (1820-1860) 81
Civil War
    (1861-1865) 103
Transition
    (1866-1871) 109
Summer Visitors, Day Trippers
    (1872-1913) 121
Changes: A Canal and a War
    (1914-1918) 155
The Modern Era
    (1919-1940) 167
Maturity
    (1941-1960) 181
New Consciousness
    (1961-1982) 191
Bibliography 220
Index 221

Our family has always been in love with Cape Cod. For us, the best mornings begin with a walk down the bleached wooden stairs to the beach, just as the summer sun is rising over Nantucket Sound. On the way to the salt marsh, you can easily recall the Wampanoags who once dug for clams and mussels along these tidal flats. You can see the fishing boats, each with a hundred gulls wheeling around, as they head out to catch cod, hake, and halibut off the Pollock Rip or farther out on the Georges Bank. You pass a shingled saltbox home, and each day you notice the last summer's cedar shingles have turned a little grayer from the salty wind off the Sound.

For thousands of years, people have worked, rested, and built their homes on this special place called Cape Cod. Marion Vuilleumier recounts the generations of those who have been fortunate enough to live here—the Indians and the Pilgrims, the fishermen and the whalers, the winter people and the summer people. The pictures and words of this book tell us of our forebears who loved the Cape before us; in these pages, we can appreciate not only the natural beauty of the Cape, but the extraordinary history of this place.

Knowledge of that history will make all of us who have loved Cape Cod come to love its land, its people, and the surrounding sea all the more.

EDWARD M. KENNEDY,
UNITED STATES SENATE

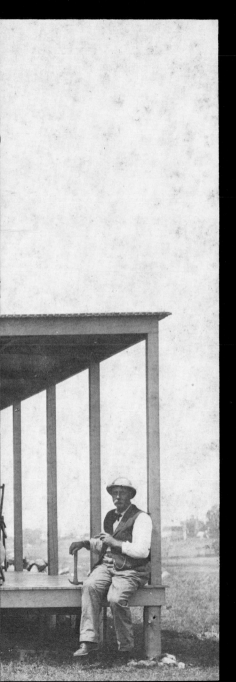

Wherein lies the magic of Cape Cod? Ever since the Pilgrims rounded the tip of this Cape and found "a good harbor," this peninsula has exerted a magnetic pull on humans.

Attached to the coast of New England by three tenuous strands—the Sagamore, Bourne, and railroad bridges—this land of ever-changing marshes, golden sands, traveling dunes, rugged pines, and ever-moving ocean has beckoned like the Lorelei of old.

Much of its charm lies in its diversity. There is something here for everyone. A many-faceted jewel, it lies glistening in its bed of blue—fascinating, tantalizing, beckoning.

Thousands caught in the machinelike grip of jobs and duties think of it as a Shangri-la, where they can relax, play, and dream. The sportsman comes to golf, fish, hunt; the sun lover to surf, swim, sail. The history buff comes to search out roots. Nature lovers hear the call of the terns, feel the fragility of the wild flowers and the endless pull of the waves. Increasing numbers of modern pilgrims have succumbed to its spell and have sought work or retired here.

Once clutched by this quaint, haunting Lorelei, another phenomenon occurs. People develop an insatiable desire to know all about it. What was it like here in the long ago? Who loved, laughed, and wept on this land? How did the many previous generations live that brought us to this day?

I hope that this collection of words and pictures will answer some of those questions.

—Marion Vuilleumier
West Hyannisport, Massachusetts

The cottage owned by Mr. Damon (left) is one of Eastham's early summer residences. The neighborhood gathering included (left to right) Frederick and Rose Fish, an unidentified couple, Mr. and Mrs. Robert Terry and Francis W. Smith.

Around the turn of the century many locals were renting cottages or providing rooms to folk escaping the hot cities. Photograph courtesy of Sadie F. Flint

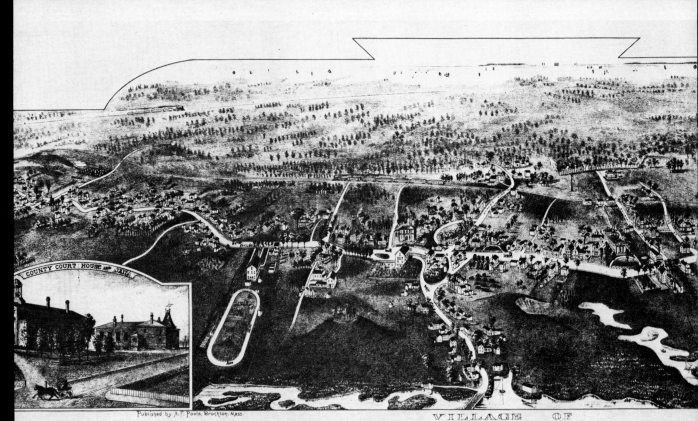

REFERENCES

A – U.S. Post Office and Custom House
B – Court House
C – County Jail
D – O.C.R.R. Depot.
E – Globe Hotel.

F – County Fair Grounds.
G – Unitarian Church.
H – Baptist Church.
L – Methodist Church.
K – Masonic Temple.

COUNTY COURT HOUSE AND JAIL.

Published by A.F. Poole, Brockton, Mass.

VILLAGE OF
BARNSTABL
·SEAT·OF·BARNSTABLE·COUNTY·MASS·
–1884.–

MARSHES PRESS

Acknowledgements

REFERENCES
L - Grammar School.
M - Cemetery.
N - Phinney & Edson - Store
O - Barnstable Patriot Office
P - Old Cemetery.

Q - Cemetery.
R - School.
S - Union Hall

Grateful appreciation is expressed to Frederick Matthews for making the initial contact and for his continued interest and help with this book.

Special thanks go to Charlotte Price, professional archivist for several Cape Cod organizations, who assisted in locating much material and many pictures.

Appreciation is expressed also to Dick Holbrook, who assisted in the collection with his photography.

Special appreciation goes to Marian Logan who took such care in typing the final manuscript.

I am grateful to many other people throughout the Cape who assisted in the collection of the illustrations. In alphabetical order they are: Patricia Anderson, Constance Andrade, Amelia Bingham, Fred Bodenseik, Harriet Ropes Cabot, Charlotte Christen, Richard Casper, F. N. Ciccone, Hugh Clark, William Chase, Kenneth Coombs, Selina Coombs, Carlton Crocker, John Howland Crocker, Rosanna Cullity, Dolores DaLuz, Wesley DeLacy, Dianne Dinger, Marilyn Fifield, Al Flint, Sadie F. Flint, Michael Frucci, Chester Frazier, Alice Gibbs, Edward Gillis, Dudley W. Hallett, Barbara Haskell, Nancy Hilmer, Stuart Iyman, Shelley Lauzon, Julius Lazarus, Stephen LeClair, Edith Linehan, Paulette Loomis, Irving Lovell, Russell Lovell, Jr., William Lowell, Greg Masterson, O. Herbert McKenney, Eric Michelson, Janet Nickerson Mott, Faith Nicholas, Edmond Rhodes Nickerson, M. Kate Olenna, Edie Parastatides, Douglas Park, Lois Palches, Peter Palches, William Quinn, Gladys Reed, Elmer Richards, Lawrason Riggs III, Karen Rinaldo, Ruth Sisson, Jack Smith, Barbara Soller, Eleanor Springer, Gordon Swan, Gertrude Tracy, Nancy Titcomb, Judson Trottier, Virginia Trottier, Helen Watt, Barbara Williams, Percy Williams.

Librarians across the Cape were as always most helpful, especially those on the staff of the Cape Cod Community College's Library Learning Resource Center. Members of the audio-visual department and the volunteers in the William Brewster Nickerson Memorial Room were most cooperative. Historical society officials in many towns were most helpful as were staff members of the Cape Cod Chamber of Commerce. I would also like to thank NASA for the satellite view of Cape Cod used on the cover.

Indians are shown playing lacrosse. Photograph from The Great Powwow *by Clara Endicot Sears; courtesy of the Cape Cod Community College Library*

Chapter 1

The
Wampanoags

thru 1620

A million years ago, the crooked peninsula of Cape Cod was a framework of sea-washed sediment built on subterranean bedrock. Then the southward-marching, mile-high glaciers deposited an untold amount of debris. Gradually, erosion attacked these high gravel beds and the endlessly working sea formed the Cape's shores.

When the first tawny-skinned people arrived many eons later (and just yesterday by geological calendars), they found a pleasing, forested home. The surrounding sea and freshwater ponds, with their communicating streams, provided daily bread. Fertile flats like the Plains of Nauset with rich soil of "blackish and deep mold" yielded vast, rippling fields of corn.

The Wampanoags, later inhabitants of this unusual land which buffers the rocky coast of New England from the vastness of the immense ocean, sensed their dependency on this gemlike soil and treated it with gentleness and respect. They moved across its face as the herring ran, the corn matured, or fish schools hugged the shores. There are no traces of earth gouging or marsh filling; only piles of shells uncovered by shifting sands, or walled, sparkling springs reveal their traces. Delicately and frugally, they used the animal world and nature's bounty, killing and using only what they needed to survive.

Around A.D. 1000, Vikings ventured westward from the *fjords* of their frigid Scandinavian homeland. They came upon a land "that had everything needful," which many believe to have been Cape Cod. A rune stone in Bourne, a sunken cellar in Provincetown, and rock markings on the shores of Follins Pond are pointed to as proof of Viking explorations. However, the Viking settlements were not permanent, and the continent went "undiscovered" for several more centuries.

Fishermen and explorers from Europe ventured westward across the turbulent Atlantic in the 1500s. One of them, Verrazano, a Florentine skipper sponsored by King Francis I of Spain, sailed into the bay south of the Cape in 1524 and found "about twenty small boats of people, which with divers cries and wonderings came toward our ship. . . . Their boats were made of one log, by the aid of fire and tools of stone, and of sufficient capacity to take care of from ten to fifteen men."

In the spring of 1602, Bartholomew Gosnold left Falmouth, England, to found a colony "in some agreeable spot, preferably where gold was abundant." Six weeks or so later, he dropped anchor off the Cape tip's outer beach. Excited by the numbers of codfish swimming about his ship, he caught an abundance and triumphantly named the projection "Cape Cod."

Ashore, he found the beach pebbles were not made of gold, so he continued exploring the coast of the Cape, then landed on what was later named Martha's Vineyard. Though his intended colony did not take root, Gosnold sailed home with a cargo of cedar and sassafras.

In 1603 Martin Pring and his crew spent seven weeks in Cape Cod Bay searching for sassafras for the French court, which had been visited with an epidemic of pox. Since the powdered root of sassafras produced perspiration, seventeenth century doctors prescribed it for this illness and many

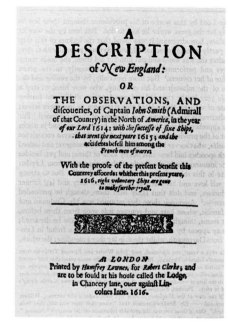

This is the frontispiece of Captain John Smith's book. Photograph from History of Plymouth Plantation *by William Bradford; courtesy of the Cape Cod Community College Library*

A part of the Champlain's map of New England shows Cape Cod as "*C. Blan.*" *Photograph from* History of Plymouth Plantation *by William Bradford; courtesy of the Cape Cod Community College Library*

others. During this period Pring and his men had several encounters with the natives, who did not come too close because of the ship's "two great and fierce mastiffs."

Two years later Samuel de Champlain dropped anchor at Nauset and found "five to six hundred savages, all naked except their loins which were covered by doe or seal skin. They wore their hair carefully combed and trussed in various ways. . . . Their bodies were well proportioned and their skin olive colored. They adorn themselves with feathers, beads of shell and other geegaws which they arrange neatly in embroidered work. As weapons they have bows, arrows and clubs. They are not so much great hunters as tillers of the soil." Champlain noted crops of corn, beans, squash, pumpkin, and tobacco.

All of these adventurers brought back to their homelands glowing reports of this new land in the western world, and serious thought was given to settlement.

This map of Nauset Harbor was drawn by Champlain. Photograph from the History of Plymouth Plantation *by William Bradford; courtesy of the Cape Cod Community College Library*

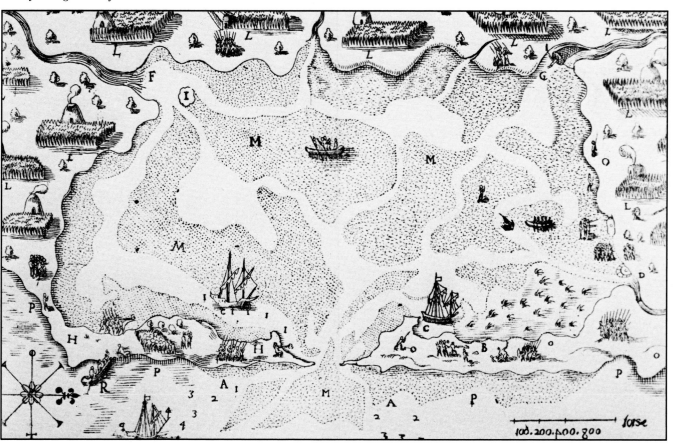

Gosnold's Arrival at Cuttyhunk, an early Dutch etching from Early History of Naushon Island *by Amelia Forbes Emerson. Photograph courtesy of the trustees of the Naushon Island Trust and the Cape Cod Community College Library*

During the summer the Wampanoags lived in homes made of bent samplings covered with bark and woven mats. These dwellings were seasonal, for the Indians moved to the shore in warm months and erected new dwellings wherever their fancy took them. Sketch by Pierre Dupont Vuilleumier; from the coloring book Along the Wampanoag Trail

The Wampanoags were skilled in basketry, using the natural reeds and grasses in the forest. Those sketched here were seen in the Wampanoag Indian Museum in Mashpee. Sketch by Pierre DuPont Vuilleumier; from the coloring book Along the Wampanoag Trail

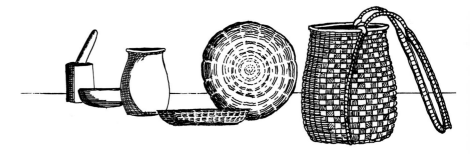

In winter several families (or generations) lived together in more permanent long houses or lodges. These were made of a double layer of bark held together with bent saplings. Sometimes seaweed was used as insulation. Fur-covered bunks lined the interior, and there was storage for baskets and utensils underneath. The fire was in the center, and a hole was above to let out the smoke. Animal skins covered the entrances. Sketch by Pierre DuPont Vuilleumier; from the coloring book Along the Wampanoag Trail

Skins of animals were dried and used as clothing and as blankets. Sketch was made from an outdoor exhibit at the Wampanoag Indian Museum in Mashpee. Sketch by Pierre DuPont Vuilleumier; from the coloring book Along the Wampanoag Trail

This Indian fish basket was made about 1930 by Eben Quippish of Mashee, "the person nearest to pure Indian ancestry" who kept alive the craft of basket making, according to the label. Photograph by Dick Holbrook; courtesy of the Trayser Museum

A seventeenth century observer of native life wrote that Indian canoes "were all made in one piece, very easy to upset... made of either Pine-trees, which they burned hollow, scraping them smooth with Clam-shels and Oyster-shels, cutting their out-sides with stone hatchets. These Boats be not above a foot and a halfe, or two feet wide, and twenty-foote long....They use Paddles and sticks with which they row faster than our Barges" (Brenizer, The Nantucket Indians). *Sketch by Pierre DuPont Vuilleumier; from the coloring book* Along the Wampanoag Trail

Captain John Smith explored the coast of New England and chronicled the beauties and riches of Cape Cod in 1614. He was most enthusiastic about the corn that opened with unexcelled speed, the abundance of furs and fish, and the varieties of game. He recorded in a small booklet the excellence of the country for any purpose and was further confident that gold and copper could easily be found. He returned to England with his hold full of fish, furs, and whale oil, proving to his compatriots that treasure was waiting beyond the horizon. *Photograph from* Historic Pilgrimages in New England *by Edward M. Bacon; courtesy of the Trayser Museum*

Shell Heaps marking the sites of Indian Settlements.

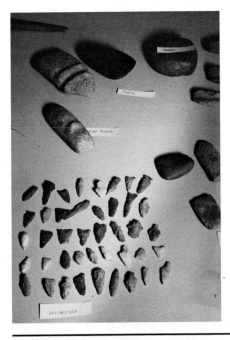

*A*rrowheads, pestle, hammer, chisel, spear head, knives, gouges, and fishing sinkers were used by the Wampanoags. Photograph by Dick Holbrook; from the Tales of Cape Cod Collection; courtesy of Trayser Museum

*I*ndians chipped pieces from this rock of pressed quartz and made arrowheads. The rock was deposited by the glacier thousands of years ago. Henry Salo found it in a Barnstable field and donated it to the museum. Photograph by Dick Holbrook; courtesy of Trayser Museum

*S*hell heaps mark the sites of Wampanoag settlements, according to an 1883 report by Henry E. Chase who wrote: "These Indians never abandoned use of wigwams for of permanent relics. Shell heaps and burial places were to a great extent obliterated places were to a great extent obliterated before sufficient intelligence and interest in their preservation were awakened." Photograph courtesy of the Cape Cod Community College Library

*T*he Nauset tribe of Wampanoag Indians, who lived in Eastham prior to Pilgrim days, sharpened their tools on this rock. The broad channels of the ancient sandstone were used to sharpen stone axes, while the nearly flat surfaces were used to grind the edges of tomahawks and chisels. Narrow grooves formed v-shaped fish bones.

Originally the rock lay on the beach at the western shore of Nauset Harbor. In recent years officials of the Cape Cod National Seashore Park moved the stone to Skiff Hill and placed it under a protective shelter. Sketch by Louis Vuilleumier; from Indians on Olde Cape Cod

Mayflower II *rounded the Cape tip on* June 12, 1957, *in a reenactment of the* 1620 *voyage. Captain Alan Viliers was master.* Mayflower II *was designed as close as possible to the original ship, which carried* 102 *passengers. It is now berthed at the state pier in Plymouth, about three miles from the reconstructed Plimoth Plantation. Visitors to the ship may hear members of the crew and passengers describe that arduous crossing. Photograph courtesy of Tales of Cape Cod, Inc.*

Chapter 2

The Pilgrims

1620-1636

When the overcrowded, storm-tossed *Mayflower* land in Plimoth (earliest spelling) on that wintry day, December 21, 1620, after an earlier landfall on the the trip of Cape Cod, a casual observer would not have considered it a treasure ship. Yet the legacy brought by the weary, half-sick Pilgrim band was of great value and became a cornerstone of our nation.

A strong religious faith and the belief that man had an inherent right to worship God according to the dictates of conscience had drawn the Pilgrims from the civilized world to a primeval wilderness. A new form of church structure was to result. In addition, their belief that all men are created equal and have a right to self-government led them to create and sign the Mayflower Compact in Provincetown Harbor. This historic document became a precursor of the Declaration of Independence and the United States Constitution.

Pilgrim leaders William Bradford, Edward Winslow, and William Brewster were determined that culture and the benefits of civilization would not be wanting in this new colony. These men, particularly Brewster, who had matriculated at Peterhouse College in Cambridge, England, had tucked into the *Mayflower* a large quantity of books.

It should immediately be said that the Pilgrims survived that first bitter winter because they were welcomed by the Wampanoags. The Great Sachem Massasoit, who headed some thirty tribute tribes in present-day southeastern Massachusetts and Rhode Island, visited Plimoth in March of 1621 to make it official. Accompanied by his brother Quadequina and sixty braves, he exchanged presents with the Pilgrims.

The first few years were spent amid adversity. The Plimoth village was built, fields were tended, sown, and harvested. Fishing and hunting skills were perfected, and some explorations were undertaken.

By 1627 the Pilgrims had established the Aptucxet Trading Post to the south of the Manomet River. In order to pay back their sponsors, a group of London merchants, the Pilgrims had to send to England large numbers of furs. The location of this trading post was strategic, for the Pilgrims could reach both the Indians and the Dutch of New Amsterdam, who had contacted them by sailing into the present Buzzards Bay. Skins of beaver, otter, mink, and muskrat soon found their way to England, and, in spite of disagreements with the sponsors, high interest rates, and discouraging harvests, the Pilgrims persisted, paying off their obligations by 1645.

In the many trips south to the trading post, the Pilgrims traveled near the extensive salt marshes south of Scusset Creek. They noted the abundant cattle fodder and the verdant, unpopulated land. Expeditions to the Cape's outer arm to buy corn from the Wampanoags had further revealed this land's suitability for homes. Already Plimoth was crowded, for many ships had brought colonists escaping the civil turmoil in England. In the late 1630s the magnetic pull of this very special land was at work.

The Compact

IN THE NAME OF GOD, AMEN. We whose names are underwritten, the loyal subjects of our dread sovereign Lord, King James, by the grace of God, of Great Britain, France and Ireland King, Defender of the Faith, etc.

Having undertaken, for the glory of God, and advancement of the Christian faith and honor of our King and Country, a voyage to plant the first colony in the northern parts of Virginia, do by these presents, solemnly and mutually in the presence of God, and one of another, covenant and combine ourselves together into a civil body politic, for our better ordering and preservation and furtherance of the ends aforesaid; and by virtue hereof to enact, constitute and frame such just and equal laws, ordinances, acts, constitutions and offices, from time to time, as shall be thought most meet and convenient for the general good of the Colony: unto which we promise all due submission and obedience.

IN WITNESS WHEREOF we have hereunder subscribed our names at Cape Cod, the 11 of November, in the year of the reign of our sovereign Lord King James; of England, France and Ireland the eighteenth, and of Scotland the fifty-fourth. Ano. Dom. 1620.

§‡John Carver,	*Richard Warren,	‡‡John Turner,	†Edmond Margeson,
§‡*William Bradford,	*John Howland,	‡*Francis Eaton,	*Peter Brown,
‡‡*Edward Winslow,	‡*Stephen Hopkins,	‡†*James Chilton,	†Richard Britteridge,
§‡*William Brewster,	‡†Edward Tilly,	§‡John Crackston,	*George Soule,
‡‡*Isaac Allerton,	‡†*John Tilly,	‡*John Billington,	†Richard Clarke,
‡‡*Myles Standish,	§*Francis Cooke,	‡*Moses Fletcher,	Richard Gardiner,
*John Alden,	§†*Thomas Rogers,	§‡John Goodman,	†John Allerton,
§*Samuel Fuller,	‡‡*Thomas Tinker,	§‡*Degory Priest,	§‡†*Thomas English,
‡ Christopher Martin,	‡‡John Rigdale,	§‡*Thomas Williams,	*Edward Doty,
‡‡*William Mullins,	‡‡*Edward Fuller,	Gilbert Winslow,	Edward Leister.
‡‡*William White,			

(Note: November 21st. of our Calendar is the same as November 11th. of the Old Style Calendar.)

* Has descendants.   ‡ Brought wife.   § From Leyden.   † Died first winter.

The Mayflower Compact, signed in Provincetown Harbor on November 21, 1620 (November 11, Old Style calendar), is the first known charter of a government of the people, by the people, and for the people. It could be considered the first American State Paper. Photograph courtesy of the Society of Mayflower Descendants

*R*everend John Robinson's prayer at the departure of the Pilgrims from Delph Haven, Holland, from an etching in Plymouth and the Pilgrims *by Joseph Banvard. Photograph courtesy of the Cape Cod Community College Library*

A gilded bas relief of the signing of the Mayflower Compact may be seen at the base of the Pilgrim Memorial Monument in Provincetown. Photograph courtesy of Bourne Town Archives

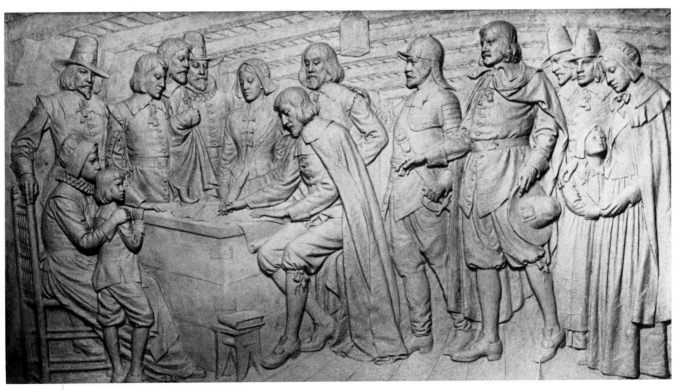

The first washing day at Cape Cod was painted by the artist Merrill. Photograph of painting from Truro, Cape Cod by Shebnah Rich; courtesy of the Cape Cod Community College Library

When the Pilgrims landed at Plimoth, their first concern was to build houses, for winter was upon them. They laid out a street, lined it with houses, and later built a fort.

The present Plimoth Plantation recreates life as it would have been lived in 1627. Men and women portray known residents of the village. A Wampanoag camp recreates Indian life of that era. *Photographs courtesy of Plimoth Plantation*

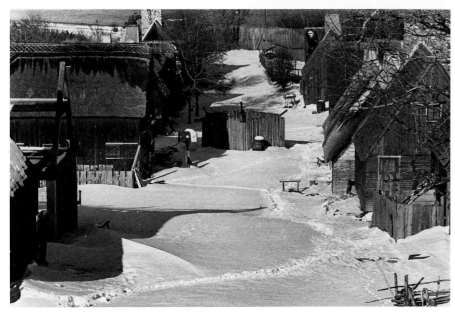

A reenactment of the Pilgrims gathering for worship at Fort Meetinghouse. Built in 1622-23, the building was designed for protection as well as for religious services. However, the natives were friendly, and the cannons on the rooftop were never fired in war. Photograph courtesy of Plimoth Plantation

The peace treaty between the Pilgrims and the Wampanoags in March 1621 was interpreted by Palo Alto Peirce of Freetown. One eyewitness described the Indians as "tall proper men" and Massasoit, their supreme sachem, as having a great chain of white bone and a long knife hanging around his neck. Another eyewitness called Massasoit "a man who possessed the elements of a great and noble mind and a generous heart."

William Bradford, who had not yet been elected governor, wrote in his journal that "after friendly entertainment and some gifts given him, they made a peace with him (Massasoit)," and that Squanto, a native of that area, "continued with them and was their interpreter and was a special instrument sent of God for their good beyond their expectation." Etching from Indian History, Biography and Genealogy; Pertaining to the Good Sachem Massasoit of the Wampanoag Tribe, and His Descendants *by Ebeneezer W. Peirce; courtesy of* Tales of Cape Cod, Inc.

The Pilgrims were taught by their Wampanoag friend, Squanto, to plant herring with corn as fertilizer, as sketched by artist Ellen Brewster from the Plimoth Colony Cookbook. *Photograph courtesy of the Plymouth Antiquarian Society*

Edward Winslow was portrayed in a painting attributed to Robert Walker. Now hanging at Pilgrim Hall in Plymouth, it is the only known picture of a Mayflower Pilgrim. *Photograph from* History of Plymouth Plantation *by William Bradford; courtesy of the Cape Cod Community College*

Governor William Bradford is shown at work on his journal. Sketch courtesy of the Governor William Bradford Compact and Mary Ellen Pogue

The Pilgrims depended on fish and shellfish along with corn to keep them alive those first hard winters. Sketch by artist Ellen Brewster, from Plimoth Colony Cookbook. Photograph courtesy of the Plymouth Antiquarian Society

This is a replica of the Aptucxet Trading Post in Bourne where the first business contract was signed in America, in 1627, about six years after the Pilgrims arrived. In it Governor William Bradford and seven other Pilgrims secured control from the Colony and from the London Adventures of trade in furs, sassafras, and lumber for six years with renewal rights. Two men lived at the post, trading with Indians and Dutch. The replica was erected in 1930, as close as possible to the original. Photograph from the Lombard Collection, of Bourne Historical Society; courtesy of Bourne Town Archives

Percival Hale Lombard (left), indefatigable historical researcher, and Nathan Bourne Hartford excavated the site of the first trading post. The location was always well-known, having been owned by one family, the Perrys, for 200 years, but the stone foundation had become overgrown. In 1930 Lombard and others in the Bourne Historical Society embarked upon extensive research, and a replica was faithfully constructed. Bowls, spoons, clay pipes, a candle holder, and a large key found during the excavations are on display. Photograph from the Lombard Collection, Bourne Historical Society; courtesy of the Bourne Town Archives

The two sides of a Spanish Netherland coin (enlarged from its one-half-inch diameter), the type used by the Pilgrims. Although this coin was not minted until 1649, this type of coin was used throughout Western Europe in the early 1600s. When they arrived in the New World, the Pilgrims found another type of coinage in use—wampum.

This coin has been in the collection of the Vuilleumier family for many years. Photographs by Dick Holbrook

This is a string of wampum, or Indian money, which was introduced to the Plimoth Colony by Isaac de Rasieres, Dutch representative from New Amsterdam (New York). Made from shells, these were smoothed with stone, drilled, and strung on thongs or on braided grass. This particular string of wampum is on view summers at the Aptucxet Trading Post and is owned by the Bourne Historical Society. Photograph from the Lombard Collection, Bourne Historical Society; courtesy of the Bourne Town Archives

Typical shell from which wampum was made. The values were as follows: six pieces of white or three pieces of blue were equal to one English penny; a "fathom of Peague" (or a string of white wampum six feet long) was worth five English shillings.

Tribute in wampum was brought to both Plimoth and Massachusetts Bay colonies by various Indian tribes. At one time every skin bought and sold suffered a tax of two pence, payable in wampum. Photograph from the Lombard Collection, Bourne Historical Society; courtesy of the Bourne Town Archives

NEVV ENGLANDS PROSPECT.

A true, lively, and experimentall defcription of that part of *America*, commonly called Nevv England: difcovering the ftate of that Countrie, both as it ftands to our new-come *Englifh* Planters; and to the old Native Inhabitants.

Laying downe that which may both enrich the knowledge of the mind-travelling Reader, or benefit the future Voyager.

By William Wood.

Printed at *London* by *Tho. Cotes*, for *Iohn Bellamie*, and are to be fold at his fhop, at the three Golden Lyons in *Corne-hill*, neere the *Royall Exchange*. 1634.

William Wood came to New England with John Endecott's party, which settled Salem in 1629. Wood traveled extensively throughout the English settlements for about four years before returning to London and producing a pleasantly informative book about the region. Photograph from New England's Prospect *by William Wood*

The South part of Nevv-England, as it is Planted this yeare, 1634.

This map shows the south part of New England as "planted" in 1634. Photograph from New England's Prospect *by William Wood*

The First Congregational Church of
Yarmouth was gathered in 1639, several
months before the incorporation of the
town. The fourth and present building was
constructed in 1879. Sketch by Pierre
DuPont Vuilleumier; from Churches of
Cape Cod

Chapter 3

An Arm of the Old Colony

Like a giant flexing his arm, Plimoth Colony spread outward. Once the surrounding towns like Duxbury and Weymouth were established, the colonists spread south. Massachusetts Bay Colony had been founded in 1630 by Governor John Winthrop and 400 Puritans from England, so expansion northward was not possible. Since the Bay Colony too was becoming crowded, the Cape was alluring to the more venturesome in both settlements.

Sandwich was the first Cape town settled by whites in 1637, when ten men of Saugus led by Edmund Freeman received permission from Governor Bradford to settle there. Those first Sandwich residents erected temporary rough huts for immediate shelter. A simple, rectangular, thatch-roofed church for worship and community meetings was the first public building. It was followed by a tannery and a blacksmith's shop. The tiny community of some sixty families was almost immediately self-sufficient. They had everything except a mill. To have corn ground, they had to travel to the Jenny mill in Plimoth.

The men farmed the land—and the sea, too—as time permitted. The women were occupied from dawn till dusk with weaving, sewing, soap making, candle making, and cooking over the enormous fireplaces. In later years the town of Bourne would "secede" and become a separate town from Sandwich.

Barnstable, the second foundation town, named for Barnstaple, England, was settled by an entire congregation. Founded in London in 1616, the Separatist parish was out of harmony with the established Church of England. In 1632 a worship service was raided and leaders jailed. Threatened with persecution, the parishioners and first minister, Reverend John Lothrop, sailed for Plimoth Colony in 1634. After a brief stay in Scituate, permission was granted for settlement on the broad marshes called by the natives "Mattackeese," and the parish moved there in 1639.

Worshiping first in the open, at a place marked by Sacrament Rock, the settlers constructed a meetinghouse and built their homes along the ancient path known first as Indian Trail, next as King's Highway, and finally as Route 6A. Eventually settlers from this town founded Falmouth.

Reverend Stephen Bachiler, a minister from Lynn, north of Boston, and England's Anthony Thacher arrived in the third foundation town of Yarmouth in 1639. With the help of the Colony arbitrator, fiery Captain Myles Standish, land was allocated to newly arriving settlers. A portion was reserved around Long Pond and the Bass River for the Wampanoags who already dwelt here. Quakers clustered together in the southern part of the town. In the future, this town would be divided and Dennis would become a reality.

The fourth white foundation settlement of Eastham included the vast territory from the Yarmouth bounds to the Cape tip, when "the vigorous half" of the Plimoth colonists arrived in the spring of 1644.

Governor Bradford noted sadly in his diary *Of Plymouth Plantation,* "Thus was this poor church (Plimoth) left, like an ancient mother grown old and forsaken of her children, though not in their affections, yet in regard of their bodily presence and personal helpfulness."

Though many of the Eastham settlers were Old Comers (passengers on the *Mayflower*, and *Fortune*, and the *Anne*) some were of the second generation. Purchasing land from natives Mattaquason, Sachem of Monomoyick (Chatham), and George, Sachem of Nauset, they laid claim as far as the Cape's tip. Full township was granted to this territory in 1646, though it was not called Eastham until 1651. Eventually Eastham was to splinter into eight towns.

While white settlers fanned outward from Plimoth Plantation, Sandwich's Richard Bourne had become concerned that the land of the Wampanoags would eventually be taken away from them. In 1638 he aided Quachatisset and other "South Sea" (Nantucket Sound) natives to register their ancient deeds with Plimoth Colony. The headquarters of this 13,500-acre tract was the home of the Mashpee (Marshpee) tribe, so it was designated the Plantation of Mashpee. When this grant or patent was ratified by the General Court in 1682, the entailment was made to the South Sea Indians and their children forever "so that no part or parcel of these lands might be bought or sold to any white person without the consent of all of the said Indians, not even with the consent of the Court."

Initially there was harmony between the races, but tension rose as the white population increased. At first the natives welcomed as guests these strangers from over the seas. They were puzzled, however, by the English custom of settling in one place and fencing off homes. Couldn't the white man see that the land was created and given by the "shining one above" and could not be individually owned? If a white man wanted to give a kettle, a hatchet, or clothing in return for a squiggle on a paper, why not oblige him? When a fence was erected and the natives were ordered off land their people had hunted on for generations, the natives were baffled and withdrew.

As the white settlements fanned out over the Cape in the 1660s, natives had the choice of living among the whites or grouping in their own neighborhoods. Gradually Wampanoags gathered in pockets up and down the peninsula. As their numbers diminished and a few intermarried, most withdrew to Mashpee, which, thanks to the foresight of Reverend Bourne and the Wampanoag chieftains, was still a native area.

There were, of course, two kinds of whites: those who took advantage of the natives, and others like Bourne, Reverend John Eliot of Roxbury, and Reverend Samuel Treat of the Outer Cape, who gave unstinting assistance to the native population. Though integration was not easy, the settling of the two races on the Cape was, in general, peacefully and quietly accomplished.

It was different off-Cape, where many new settlers who did not have the Pilgrim's religious and moral convictions had arrived. These newer arrivals were encroaching on the traditional native hunting and fishing grounds and settling nearer and nearer to tribal villages. Many of the later English arrivals were not aware of the earlier treaty and did not have the respect and friendship the Wampanoags accorded to the inhabitants of Pilgrim towns.

After Massasoit's death in 1661, Wamsutta, the eldest son, became Great Sachem for a brief time until he died in 1664. Then Pometecom (Metacomet), second son of Massasoit, called Philip by the English, became Great Sachem. At the age of twenty-four Pometecom had donned the "royalties" of the Wampanoag ruler, which included a stole, headband, breastplate, and scarlet cloak. Outwardly friendly to the English, he was inwardly torn because there were "hawks" in his council who advocated war before the Wampanoags became extinct. Philip confided to an English friend, John Borden: "But little remains of my ancestors' domain. I am resolved not to see the day when I have no country." He did, however, confirm his father's peace treaty at the conference in the Taunton meetinghouse in 1671.

But grievances mounted. Settlers did not respect the native corn fields, which by custom were not fenced. "Firewater" caused havoc. Philip somberly watched while his territory was eroded. The colonists' need and greed for land encouraged the natives' desire for kettles, beads, cloth, and knives.

On June 10, 1675, the short and bloody King Philip's War began. Hostilities started in Swansea and gradually engulfed most of Massachusetts. On the Cape, though, there was peace. White and tan inhabitants had always had friendly relations, so the local Indians did not answer Philip's call to arms. Elsewhere, after savagery was committed by both sides, skirmishes intensified. Gradually the settlers, with their greater numbers and better arms, prevailed. Fourteen months later, Philip lay dead at Mount Hope, and the Wampanoags were almost exterminated. Only Mashpee on Cape Cod and Gay Head on Martha's Vineyard remained official native towns.

Another less bloody but equally fateful transition was to occur in the Old Colony a few years later.

While Thomas Hinckley of Eastham was in his sixth term as governor of Plimoth Colony, King James II of England capriciously decided to abolish colonial self-government. In 1686 he sent the notorious Edmund Andros to be royal governor. Announcing that colonists were not true Englishmen, Andros declared farm titles invalid and Indian deeds worthless. One can imagine the dismay of the entire colony.

Hinckley was in no position to oppose Andros, who represented the might of the Crown, so he accepted a seat on the Colony Council in order to mediate, but he had little success. A bruising tax program began and citizens bristled at the oppression.

When James II fled the throne and William and Mary became the English rulers, the colonists immediately deposed and jailed Andros, installing Hinckley as governor again.

Earlier, under Hinckley's able leadership and wise administration, plans had been made to arrange the far-flung settlements into three counties. In 1685 Plymouth, Bristol, and Barnstable counties were created. The latter consisted of the entire Cape, with Barnstable as the shire town. A courthouse was built and county officials were designated.

Any hope for easing the strain between Crown and the Colonies was soon gone though, for William and Mary could not be persuaded to give charts in New England to both Plimoth and its northern neighbor on Massachusetts Bay.

Despite bitter protests from residents in both colonies, in 1692 Plimoth Colony and Massachusetts Bay Colony were united by the English Parliament into the royal province of Massachusetts Bay. Furthermore, the Crown insisted on continuing the royal governors. The idyllic period when colonists were left pretty much on their own was ended. The tax program was pursued more vigorously by King and Parliament. The seeds of the American Revolution were sown.

The First Church of Christ in Sandwich was "gathered" along with the town when "ten men of Saugus" were granted land for settlement in late 1637. The present building was erected in 1847 and is a graceful colonial-style structure with a steeple similar to one designed in London by Sir Christopher Wren. Photograph courtesy of the Cape Cod Chamber of Commerce

By 1630 Puritans from England had settled the Massachusetts Bay Colony in Boston. As each colony received more settlers and new towns were begun, the questions of the boundary between the two colonies arose.

In 1644 a commission from each colony was chosen to mark the actual boundary, which was supposed to be at the furthermost part of the Charles River. After tramping through the woods, the men found themselves slightly off course.

Rather than retrace their steps, they created an angle, using a large tree as a marker. This original "angle tree" stood for some 150 years until it finally decayed.

The Angle Tree Stone (pictured here) was erected by vote of the Commonwealth of Massachusetts in 1790 "to perpetuate the place on which the late station or Angle Tree formerly stood." The photograph was taken in the 1940s as William Chase gazed at the monument.

The slate monument still marks the boundary between Plainville and North Attleboro, Massachusetts, and Cumberland, Rhode Island. It is pictured on the logo of the town of Plainville. Currently the marker is under protective covering while the North Attleboro Historical Society seeks funds to give it a permanent protective structure. Photograph by Ray Fulton; donated by Barbara Fulton Parminter; courtesy of the Plainville Historical Commission

One of Sandwich's oldest houses is the Hoxie House, which overlooks the quiet waters of Shawme Pond. The weathered, shingled salt box was occupied by Reverend John Smith and his family from 1655 to 1688, though a brick from the chimney is dated earlier. The house was named for Captain Abraham Hoxie, a whaling captain who owned it in the 1800s. The town acquired the old home in 1959 and restored it. Visitors in summer can see how people lived in the 1676-1680 period, for the Hoxie House has authentic furnishings. Sketch by Louis Vuilleumier; from Sketches of Cape Cod

Coopers at work, from an engraving in William Bradford's History of Plymouth Plantation. Photograph courtesy of the Cape Cod Community College Library

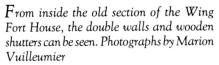

From inside the old section of the Wing Fort House, the double walls and wooden shutters can be seen. Photographs by Marion Vuilleumier

Wing Fort House dates to 1641 and is not only the town of Sandwich's oldest house, but it has been owned and lived in continuously by Wing descendants for three centuries. The right front section was built as a refuge from possible Indian attack, tradition says. Purchased by the Wing Family of America from the last Wing occupant in 1842, the house is now a museum, open in the summer for visitors. Photograph by Marion Vuilleumier

In 1652-3 there was a scarcity of coin, so the inhabitants of Sandwich were assessed taxes in butter. Part of the festivities of the Wing reunion in 1902 was the Butter Parade, in which the entire family paraded to the Town Hall and presented the selectmen with a wooden firkin containing thirty pounds of dairy butter. John Mansir Wing of Chicago is custodian of the butter barrow in this picture. The ladies are Mrs. George Wing Sisson (left) and Miss Angela Wing. There were 300 Wings present. Photograph courtesy of the Wing Family of America

Tradition places the first service of the church members at Sacrament, or Pulpit Rock, when the town of Barnstable was established in 1639. Until the early part of this century Sacrament Rock, pictured here in 1897, stood by the roadside. When the state road (Route 6A) was built, the rock was directly in the path and was dynamited. Pieces were cemented together and placed on the north side of the road in the approximate location of the first service. Photograph courtesy of John Howland Crocker

Sturgis Library
Barnstable, Mass.
Richard Sears Gallagher '59

Barnstable's earliest standing house is now the front section of the Sturgis Library on Route 6A. Built in 1644 for the town's first minister, it was used for church services until the first meetinghouse was built. The Lothrop Room, on the right first floor in this picture, has the Lothrop Bible on display.

The home was the birthplace of William Sturgis, who went to sea at the age of fifteen and made a fortune sending clipper ships to trade in China and this country's Northwest. Sturgis gave the house to the town for use as a library. Sketch by Richard Sears Gallagher; courtesy of the Sturgis Library

The West Parish Meetinghouse in West Barnstable was founded before the town was established. The parish was formed in England in 1616, and thirty members and Pastor Lothrop went to Scituate. Members moved to the Great Marshes of Barnstable in 1639 and founded the town.

The first meetinghouse was erected in 1634. After east and west parishes were established in 1717, this colonial-style church was built. Parishioners in the east section of the town established the church on Cobb's Hill, now Unitarian Universalist. Photograph courtesy of the Cape Cod Chamber of Commerce

The eastern view of Yarmouth prior to 1839 as seen in the John Warner Barber collection of information about each Massachusetts town. Photograph courtesy of the Cape Cod Community College Library

Building the Schooner, an etching from the South Sea Whaler by W. H. G. Kingston, is evidence that colonists soon took to the sea to earn a living. Photograph courtesy of the Cape Cod Community College Library

Many sailors from Cape Cod experienced shipwreck. Some, like these pictured in the South Sea Whaler by W. H. G. Kingston, were saved from starvation by the birds. Photograph courtesy of the Cape Cod Community College Library

Thomas Prence (or Prince), who arrived on the ship Fortune in November of 1621, was chosen governor in 1634 and again in 1638. According to tradition, Prence "removed" from Duxbury to Eastham in 1640 or 1645. He brought with him from England a seedling of a pear tree that flourished for 200 years. In 1839 "the fruit is small but excellent; and it yields, upon the average, fifteen bushels of fruit," according to John Warner Barber in his Historical Collections.

Governor Prence's farm comprised 200 acres just over the present town line and close to the shore. In Barber's time the farm was owned by Nathan Kenny. The original pear tree is long gone. Photograph from A Trip Around Cape Cod by E. G. Perry; courtesy of the Cape Cod Community College Library

Though no original home stands from the first settlement, this ancient house in Eastham gives an indication of what the houses were like. Photograph from A Trip Around Cape Cod by E. G. Perry; courtesy of the Cape Cod Community College Library

*T*he Old Indian Church, the oldest ecclesiastical structure on Cape Cod, originated with a gift of hand-hewn lumber given by English philanthropists. Constructed and dedicated in 1684, the church was testimony that the Cape Cod Wampanoags and their English neighbors remained peaceful during the terrible conflict known as the King Philip's War. Though originally Congregational, it later housed a Baptist group. Sketch by Pierre DuPont Vuilleumier; from Churches of Cape Cod

WAMPANOAG INDIAN TRIBES
ON
CAPE COD AND THE ISLANDS

MEESHAWN
PAMET
PONONAKANET
PATUXET
NAUSET
SCUSSET
NAMSKAKET
COMASSAKUMKANIT
TONSET
MANAMET SHAUME
SAUQUATUCKET
SKANTON
NOBSCUSSET
POKESIT
POTANUMAQUUT
KITTEAUMUT
MATTACHEESET
MATTACHEESE
MONOMOYICK
MAHAGANSETT
SANTUIT
HOCKANUM
ASHUMET MISTIC CHEQUAKET
PAWKUNNAWKUT
CHAPAQUIT MASSIPEE WIANNO
SIPPERWISSETT COTUIT COTACHESET
WAKOQUOET
POPPONESSIT
QUISSET WESQUEB
TATAKET
NOBSQUE

CHRISTIANTOWN
NUNPAUG
CHAPPAQUIDDICK
TAKEMMY
MEDAKET
SIASCONSET
AQINNAH

N
E
W
S

PIERRE DUPONT VUILLEUMIER

Dates of Incorporation of Fifteen Towns in Barnstable County (Some were settled earlier than their incorporation.)

Sandwich	1639
Barnstable	1639
Yarmouth	1639
Eastham	1651
Falmouth	1686
Harwich	1699
Truro	1709
Chatham	1712
Provincetown	1727
Wellfleet	1763
Dennis	1793
Orleans	1797
Brewster	1803
Mashpee	1870
Bourne	1884

*O*ne of the two major problems facing both Pilgrims and Indians was the ownership of land.

This map shows the distribution of the Wampanoag tribes in early Pilgrim days. Note that one town (Christiantown) had been established on Martha's Vineyard for those natives who had accepted Christianity and wished to follow the white man's way of life. Others were being established south of Boston by John Eliot. These were called Praying Indian towns.

As more and more English settlers arrived, the problem of land became acute. Map by Pierre DuPont Vuilleumier; from Indians on Olde Cape Cod

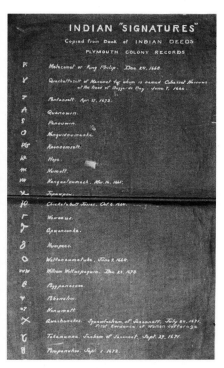

Since the Wampanoags had no written language, they used signs as signatures. These were used on deeds, treaties, and any other official documents. Plimoth Colony records include many such, and samples are recorded here. Photograph from the Lombard Collection, Bourne Historical Society; courtesy of the Bourne Town Archives

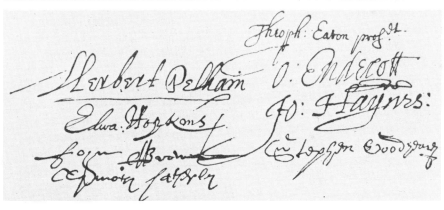

In witness wherof the parties above named have interchaingablie subscribed these presents, the day and year above writen.

JOHN WINTHROP, President. PESSECOUSS his mark
HERBERT PELHAM. MEEKESANO his mark
THO: PRENCE. WITOWASH his mark C C C
JOHN BROWNE. AUMSEQUEN his mark
GEO: FENWICK. *the Niantick deputy.*
EDWA: HOPKINS. ABDAS his mark A O
THEOPH: EATON. PUMMASH his mark
STEVEN GOODYEARE. CUTCHAMAKIN his mark [1]

The other problem facing both Pilgrims and settlers was the constant warring between Indian tribes. As the tribes were pressed inland by the newcomers, they pressed against territory of other tribes. In 1634 the plantations of Plimoth, Boston, Hartford, and New Haven formed the United Colonies of New England to protect themselves against possible war and to deal fairly with Indian problems.

Massasoit's people were still loyal, but the powerful Narragansetts and the mighty Mohicans were resentful of the colonists.

On August 27, 1645, a treaty was signed by the eight United Colonies commissioners and was marked by eight Indian chiefs. Photograph from the History of Plymouth Plantation by William Bradford; courtesy of the Cape Cod Community College Library

These candlesticks were made from the oak tree under which Reverend John Eliot preached to the Indians beginning in 1651. A bronze plaque was placed at the spot in South Natick when the tree was removed. Reverend Lewis Arthur Chase, pastor at South Natick, had a section of the tree saved and sawed into three planks. One was made into a cross for his church, one was given to Andover Newton Theological Seminary, and the other was given to Mr. A. L. McKenzie, who made the candlesticks on his lathe. Pierre Vuilleumier purchased them in 1933. Photograph by Dick Holbrook; from the Vuilleumier collection

The plaque commissioned by the Congregational Association depicts Reverend John Eliot preaching to the Indians. Though ministering in the Boston area, Eliot did visit outlying Indian towns. In July 1666, Eliot, Governor Prince, Magistrate Thomas Southworth, and several others came to Sandwich to talk with Richard Bourne and Indian church leaders about making the Mashpee parishioners into a fully constituted congregation.

On the favorable recommendation of this committee, representatives of all the colony churches gathered in Mashpee to formally constitute the church. The Indians then chose Bourne as their pastor. Eliot journeyed to the Cape again to celebrate Bourne's ordination on August 17, 1670. At the impressive ceremony Eliot, Reverend John Cotton of Plymouth, a Natick Indian church member, and a Martha's Vineyard Christian Indian performed the "laying on of hands." From Pilgrim Deeds and Duties 1620-1920, published by the Pilgrim Press

THE LORD'S PRAYER IN THE WAMPANOAG INDIAN DIALECT

"N&shun Keesukqut quttiannatanmunach k&wesunonk. Peyaum utch kukketaff &tamonk, kuttenantamoonk ne&n&nach okheit neane kesukqut. Nummeetsuongash askesutkokish assamainnean yeuyey keesukok. Kah ahquoan tamaiinnean nummatcheseongash, neane matchenenukqueagig nutaquontamounnong. Ahquc sakompagunnaiinnean en en gutchhuaouganit, webe phoquokwussinnean wuth matchitut. Newutche kutahtaunn keetass &tamonk, kah menuhkesuonk, kah sohsumoonk mickene, Amen . . . "

(The ampersand (&) represents an Indian vowel sound not reproducible by any english letter.)

A LITERAL TRANSLATION:

"Father ours above in heaven. Admired in highest manner be thy name. Like done thy will on earth as like in Heaven. Let us be forgiven evil doings of ours, as we would forgive wrong-doers to us. Not guide us into snares, but help us to escape from evil. Thine thy powerful kingdom, thine the strength, thine the greatest glory, Always, always wish me so. Amen."

This Wampanoag version of the Lord's Prayer was used in the early seventeenth century by Reverends Richard Bourne, Thomas Mayhew, Jr., Samuel Treat, John Eliot, and Roger Williams in their work with the Wampanoags of Plimoth and Massachusetts Bay colonies, as well as Providence Plantation. Prayer from Indians of Olde Cape Cod

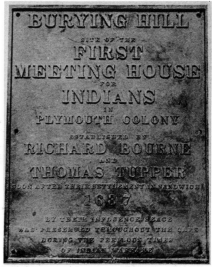

Though no longer standing today, the first Indian meetinghouse in the Colony was established in 1637 at Bournedale by Richard Bourne and Thomas Tupper. This marker was dedicated July 4, 1924, on the original site by the Bourne Historical Society. Photograph from the booklet Cape Cod, *published in 1926 by the Bourne Historical Society; courtesy of the Bourne Town Archives*

AN INDIAN VILLAGE

An etching of an Indian Village during the period of the King Philip's War, when natives had to draw close together for protection. Photograph from The Great Powwow *by Clara Endicot Sears*

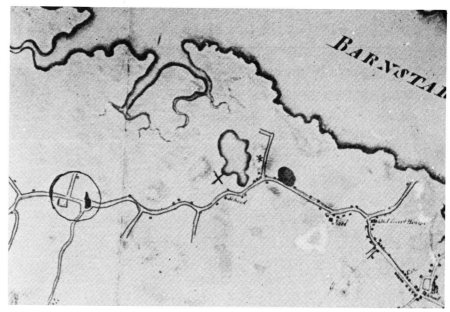

Remnants of the earliest known jail in Plimoth Colony and one of the oldest wooden prison structures in New England can be found in Barnstable on the grounds of the Trayser Museum. Built around 1690, when Barnstable was a newly created county of the Colony, it housed prisoners sentenced by the court in that town. It is made of heavy oak post and plank construction and was part of a barn before being moved to its present site on Route 6A, near the Trayser Museum. Sketch by Louis Vuilleumier; from Sketches of Cape Cod

The Colonel John Thacher House on Route 6A in Yarmouth Port is one of the few standing from the Colony period. Built in 1680 on Shore Road, it was moved to its present site later. The Thachers were among the town's first settlers, having sailed from England in 1635, been in a fierce wreck which took four of their children, and spent a year in Marblehead.

Now owned by the Society for the Preservation of New England Antiquities, the house proudly displays an old oak cradle and a scarlet coverlet which the original Thachers brought from England. The house is named for the second generation John Thacher who became an army officer. Photograph from The Collection of the Two Hundred Fiftieth Anniversary of the Founding of Yarmouth; courtesy of Jack Smith

Barnstable's Thomas Hinckley, who was both the sixth and the eighth governor of the Plimoth Colony, lived across the road (now Route 6A) from Coggins (or Hinckley's) Pond. Though the actual house site is not known, there is a roadside marker to locate the neighborhood.

Because of Hinckley's statesmanship, colonists were protected with a type of title insurance. When Sir Edmund Andros was sent to be governor (the seventh) by the Crown, he declared that titles to all lands purchased from Indians were invalid and not legally binding. Andros demanded that colonists pay quit-claim rent. In 1685, a year before Andros arrived, Hinckley had placed on record a confirmatory grant under the seal of the Colony which gave "full Assurance & Absolute Confirmation of all sd Lands, forever." Photograph from Barnstable A Bit of Nostalgia by Mary Sprague; courtesy of the Trayser Museum

The typical Cape Cod house developed in the Colony period. This house, which stood on Route 28 in Yarmouth, is a three-quarter Cape (two windows on one side of the door and one on the other). Full Capes have two windows on each side of the door, and half Capes have two windows on one side of the door. There is even a tiny quarter Cape in Sandwich which has one door and one window.

Timothy Dwight, who traveled by stagecoach around the peninsula about 1800, noted that the Cape Cod houses have "one story and four rooms on the lower floor; and are covered on the sides, as well as the roofs, with pine shingles, eighteen inches in length. The chimney is in the middle, immediately behind the front door, and on each side of the door there are two windows. The roof is straight; under it are two chambers; and there are two larger and two smaller windows in the gable end. This is the general structure of...houses from Yarmouth to Race Point....Generally they exhibit a tidy, neat aspect in themselves and in their appendages." Photograph copyright Julius Lazarus, Hyannis Massachusetts

The Old Yarmouth Inn, the Cape's oldest hostelry, has been welcoming travelers since 1696. Built as a wayside staging inn, it has had many owners. Today the Peros family continues the three-century-old tradition. Photograph by Dick Holbrook; courtesy of the Peros family

Mills began to appear by Cape brooks and
streams in this period. The first was
Dexter's Mill in Sandwich, built in 1654
by Thomas Dexter, one of the town's
founders. Fully restored in 1961, it is open
daily in summer, and visitors may see corn
ground between the ancient mill stones.
Photograph courtesy of the Cape Cod
Chamber of Commerce

This venerable example of a Cape Cod windmill is reputed to have been built in Plymouth in 1688 then ferried across the bay to Truro about 1788. Moved to Eastham just off Route 6 in 1793, it is the Cape's oldest wind-driven mill. It is restored to working condition and open for visitors in summer. Photograph from A Trip Around Cape Cod *by E. G. Perry; courtesy of the Trayser Museum*

Harvesting the hay on the Great Marshes of Barnstable was an early occuption, though this picture was taken much later, in the mid-1800s. Photograph from A Trip Around Cape Cod by E. F. Perry; courtesy of the Trayser Museum

The Great Marshes of Barnstable were a wonderful source of cattle fodder. The hay was placed on pilings until it was needed. The dunes of Sandy Neck are visible in the distance. Photograph from A Trip Around Cape Cod by E. G. Perry; courtesy of the Trayser Museum

The Wheel of Thyme Herb Garden at the entrance to the Botanic Trails of the Historical Society of Old Yarmouth was designed and planted by Barbara and William Soller of Yarmouth Port.

Herb gardens date to the very early days on the Cape, and there are gardens at the Aptucxet Trading Post in Bourne, the Hoxie House in Sandwich, and on the grounds of the Falmouth Historical Society, to name just a few. In addition, the Sollers have designed an herb garden in the shape of a cross for St. David's Episcopal Church in South Yarmouth. Photograph by William Soller

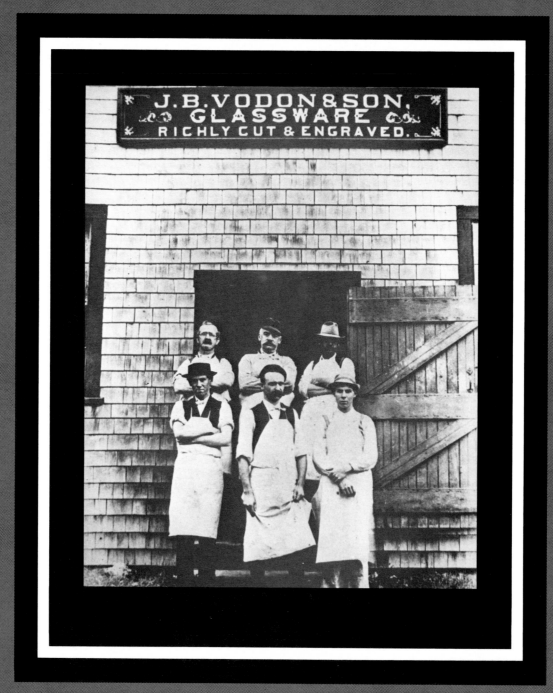

J. B. VODON & SON, GLASSWARE CO.
RICHLY CUT & ENGRAVED.

Built in the 1740s, this building on an East Sandwich pond off Route 6A was first a gristmill. Then it became a sash and blind shop. It was next a stave mill shop where barrels were made for the Boston and Sandwich Glass Company. In the later 1800s it became this glassware shop operated by the Vodon family, who cut, engraved, and decorated glass to order. Front right, a Hoxie; back left, George Harrison; back right, William Wright; all others are Vodons. Photograph from Ben Harrison; courtesy of Russell Lovell, Jr.

Chapter 4

Massachusetts vs. the Crown

1693–1819

The unique architecture and the many small industries that make the Cape's heritage so charming developed quietly during these next decades. A series of off-Cape military expeditions against the French and Indians during the Colonial wars occasionally interrupted, but failed to hinder local progress. Though militiamen answered military calls and many a local seafarer manned the whaleboats which ferried the troops, the roots of the Cape culture continued inexorably to deepen and expand.

Houses became larger, two-story, more permanent structures, and many of these homesteads were to become architectural treasures. These old patriarchs were constructed by hand, well tempered with sweat and toil.

The Hoxie and Seth Pope houses, Nye Homestead, and Skiffe House in Sandwich are notable examples. At least three of these were built earlier, but metamorphosed into grander structures in the 1700s. The Josiah Dennis Manse in Dennis, Brewster's Dillingham House, Chatham's Atwood House, and Falmouth's Saconesset Homestead stand as glowing reminders of an earlier age.

Mills for grinding corn had been built over streams and on the windswept meadows. This early major industry began because the hand grinding of corn kernels was such as arduous task. Since 1654 the Dexter mill in Sandwich had been busily grinding corn with waterpower from the Shawme stream. Other mills were operated by streams in Barnstable, Yarmouth, Brewster, Eastham, and Truro. Wind power was more available, and settlers, recalling the picturesque windmills of Holland, soon sought millwrights who could erect these long-armed sentinels in every community.

In the early 1700s the sea was as important as the land in providing food and jobs. In addition to fishing for cod and mackerel and reaping clams, oysters, and other diet staples from the seas, the colonists did battle with whales, those leviathans of the deep that often skirted the shores.

Like their native American neighbors, the colonists sought the blackfish, small first cousins of the whales, when their schools came into the sheltered bays. Blackfish were prized for the "melons" in their heads which contained valuable oil. The larger right whales were less common but as highly sought.

Cape Codders also made a living on the sea with packet boats, when canny settlers noted that it was easier to send their goods fifty water miles to Boston than three land miles to the south shore. Any overland journey was by foot, horseback, or stagecoach. The few bridges were poorly constructed. No wonder people preferred the much-more-comfortable ocean travel.

These packets were nautical schools for many youths who began their careers as deck hands coiling ropes at dockside and ended as masters of packets as well as of ships that roved the seven seas. Later these sailing ships became a mainstay of the Cape economy.

Though innkepers had welcomed travelers on Cape Cod in Pilgrim days, taverns and inn buildings did not evolve until later. The first innkeepers, or "keepers of ordinaries," slept and fed the weary guests in their homes. Anthony Thacher was the first "keeper of the ordinary" in Yarmouth, being authorized to "draw wine" in 1644. John Crocker received his license to house and feed guests in his Barnstable home in 1694.

When stagecoaches began lumbering down the old Indian Trail, known by then as "King's Highway," many innkeepers had added special ells for guests. By the mid-1700s spacious inns (the term "ordinary" was falling into disuse) and taverns, such as Crocker's in Barnstable and Fessenden's in Sandwich, were built.

Crossroads emerged in this land of dunes, sea, and forest, wherever homes clustered together in the tiny villages. At the center was always a meetinghouse, where neighbors met to worship on Sunday and where they also gathered to decide temporal matters at town meetings. Usually these simple, rectangular structures also housed the first schools.

In this time of growth, the Congregational churches of the Pilgrim tradition predominated. Three plainer Quaker structures at Sandwich, West Falmouth, and South Yarmouth bore witness to the coming of the Society of Friends. Baptists had also arrived by this time, stirred by the Great Awakening as well as the preaching of Jonathan Edwards and George Whitfield. A growing and diverse population settled into an ecumenical pattern that set the tone for the diversity of later years.

Only a handful of architectural church treasures remain from that period. One may still see the venerable 1717 Congregational meetinghouse of the West Parish Church in West Barnstable, now United Church of Christ, which was designed in the early tradition, with the entrance and the pulpit on the broadside.

Fittingly, the Cape's oldest ecclesiastical structure is the old Indian Church in Mashpee. It stood first on Briant's Neck on Santuit Pond, built in 1684 with hand-hewn lumber sent from England by the Society for Propagating the Gospel among the Indians of North America. In 1717 the church was moved to the present location on Route 28. Eventually the congregation became Baptist. Twice restored and surrounded by an ancient native burial ground, it stands as a reminder of the Wampanoags and their traditions.

Concurrent with this time of growth there was an increasing undercurrent of resentment toward the mother country. Two bruising wars between England and her daughter colonies interrupted the development of this fragile peninsula. Though the major scenes of battle were far away, a land which earned its livelihood mostly by the sea could not escape the havoc caused by guns, embargoes, and blockades.

In 1765, according to the first recorded census, there were 12,127 citizens living under the Cape's sturdy roof beams. Among these people were the men and women who became leaders in the titanic struggle for independence.

Perhaps the most outstanding of these was James Otis, Jr., the brilliant and fiery Boston lawyer who was born in 1725 in the family homestead on the great marshes of Barnstable. Called the Firebrand of the American Revolution, Otis was a prime mover in the events that moved the Cape from its period of growth into the American Revolution.

In 1761 Otis the Patriot had predicted the trouble to come in his famous speech in Boston against the British Writs of Assistance. This alerted the colonists to watch Parliament closely for any signs of other tyrannical legislation. A second effect was to split citizens into two factions—Loyalists and Patriots. Sometimes arguments over remaining loyal to the crown or becoming an independent nation split families as well as communities.

Cape settlers really became aroused in 1774 when Parliament authorized sheriffs to appoint jurors rather than to have their names drawn by selectmen as before. Committees of Correspondence, which now had been formed throughout Massachusetts Bay Colony, called for citizens to close the courts until the Crown restored these rights.

On September 26, off-Cape citizens met with Cape people at Sandwich and organized a protest march to stop the court from sitting at Barnstable. A crowd of several thousand had gathered by the next day. Dr. Nathaniel Freeman of Sandwich led the orderly march to Barnstable and the confrontation with Chief Justice James Otis, father of the Patriot, at the 1772 Colonial Courthouse.

Bowing to the obvious majority, and no doubt inwardly pleased, Otis called off the court; and the justices, including Otis, signed a promise not to assist in carrying "unconstitutional Acts into execution, nor hold any commission in consequence of said Acts." After erecting a Liberty Pole, the still-orderly procession returned to Sandwich. Their final act was to secure confessions from a trio of Tories (Loyalists) in Sandwich, who had cut down the Liberty Pole, and to force Dr. Benjamin Bourne to promise publicly to sell no more tea.

Less than a year later, when the call to arms came in April 1775, sixty-three men under Colonel Joseph Otis, brother of the Patriot, left for Boston to aid Regulars and Provincials in the siege. By this time the population had grown to more than 15,000, and many men took part in the ensuing military struggle.

Though Patriots were a vocal majority and the towns sent men and money to aid the Continental Army, there were still many who were loyal to the King. Some left their homeland forever when Boston fell, sailing in British ships to Nova Scotia or England. Others fled to Tarpaulin Cove on Naushon Island, which is off the southwestern tip of the Cape and was headquarters for the British fleet. Still others remained, eventually transferring their loyalty to the new nation.

The Barnstable County Militia became a strong force. Many of its members were chosen for the military draft. Others stayed to protect the shipping, man the farms, and defend the many miles of unprotected shores. Invasion was expected daily as British sails were seen off the bays and headlands. Provincetown, being extremely vulnerable, was continually raided by English seamen seeking food.

The only major land battle occurred at Falmouth in April 1779, when ten British vessels attempted to land soldiers in force. County militia joined the Falmouth home guard in repulsing the soldiers with brisk musket fire. Major Joseph Dimmock was a forceful leader in Falmouth's Revolutionary tribulations.

In the waning years of the war, Chatham was the scene of the only naval engagement off Cape Cod. On June 20, 1782, a British privateer quietly sailed into the harbor and seized a brigantine, a schooner, and a sloop whose crews were ashore. An alarm gun alerted fifty locals, mostly militia, who kept up such a constant fire that the British were thwarted.

Women played an important role, as always, in the life of this land, and they were especially active during the war years. They managed the young, ran the households, and brought in the crops while the men were off to the wars. But not all women were confined to traditionally female activities. Mercy Otis Warren of Barnstable, a brilliant woman and sister of the Patriot, became a leader in the struggle for independence with her pen. Tutored along with her brothers by Reverend Jonathan Russell of the West Parish Church, she eventually married her brother's Harvard classmate, James Warren of Plymouth. He became a militia colonel and president of the Provincial Congress. Thus Mercy had a unique observation post as sister, wife, and daughter of patriots and as an intimate of Revolutionary leaders, including the Washingtons and the Adamses. This daughter of the Cape was the pen woman of the American Revolution and representative of many who contributed their talents to the development of the new country.

The end of the American Revolution left the economy and the people exhausted. But soon ships were built and Cape men were ranging the seven seas. The Napoleonic wars in Europe gave Yankees immediate and lucrative trading opportunities. Pacific and West Indian traders also welcomed the American ships.

But a blow fell which was to shatter the Cape's economy. President Thomas Jefferson's Embargo Act of 1807, which preceded the War of 1812, was enacted. This immediately idled Cape sailors again, and the Declaration of War finished any semblance of shipping. This unpopular war, which lasted from 1812 to 1814, left Cape Cod vulnerable. A repetition of British activity in the Revolution followed, only with a different cast and settings.

Committees of Safety in the towns struggled with the question of buying exemption from attack or fighting. Most refused to pay tribute to the British. Again the militia played a key role in home defense when the British raided the shores.

According to Barnstable tradition, when Captain Richard Raggot of His Majesty's Ship *Spencer* demanded $6,000 in tribute, Loring Crocker brought cannon by ox team from Boston to protect his saltworks on the Common Fields. Perhaps the sight of them caused the *Spencer* to sail away. Two of these cannon may still be seen poised by the imposing 1832 courthouse.

On December 14, 1814, Captain Raggot demanded a contribution of $1,000 for the preservation of the saltworks in Orleans. When the townsfolk peremptorily declined to pay, the British attempted to land at Rock Harbor on December 19. The militia vigorously repulsed the invaders in a lively battle.

Blockade running, the capturing of crews of the grounded British frigates like the famous *Somerset*, and the firing on Falmouth by the British brig *Nimrod* kept Cape men busy. In addition, return raids on Tarpaulin Cove, again a favorite resort of British cruisers, caused much excitement. Occasionally a bounty of rice, cotton, or indigo came ashore in a captured privateer, to the joy of the residents.

There was great rejoicing locally when the peace treaty of December 24, 1814, was proclaimed. The fishing, coasting, merchant shipping, salt making, and other important occupations were resumed.

In 1755, in spite of rumblings against the mother country, appointments to certain offices were still made by the King. Here is an actual appointment of Timothy Bourne, dated January 8, 1755, to be coronor in the county of Barnstable. The appointment is signed by Governor William Shirley and testified to by Silvanus Bourne and John Otis, councillors. Photograph by Dick Holbrook; courtesy of the Bourne Town Archives

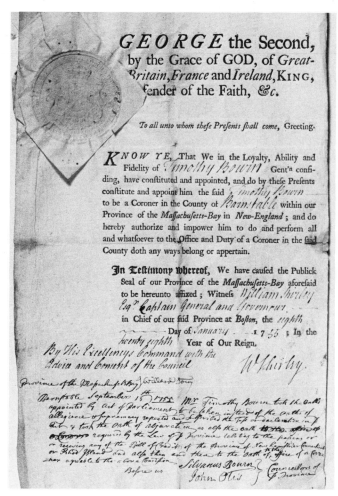

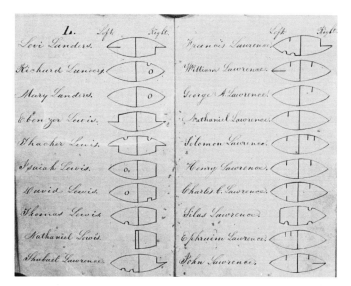

One page from the Sheep Ears Marks book at the Falmouth Historical Society records the marks branded into the sheep's ears before they were turned loose for the summer. Prior to whaling and coastal shipping days, the people of Falmouth earned their living primarily by sheep farming. This rare volume contains the brands of each family in town and dates to the 1700s. Photograph by Dick Holbrook; courtesy of the Falmouth Historical Society

Since the 1750s, Provincetown has used the services of a town crier. Until 1869, when the Provincetown Advocate newspaper began, the town crier was the only reliable source of news for the average citizen. In recent years the post of town crier has continued for the enjoyment of tourists. Postcard published for the Provincetown Advocate; courtesy of the Trayser Museum

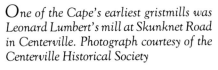

One of the Cape's earliest gristmills was Leonard Lumbert's mill at Skunknet Road in Centerville. Photograph courtesy of the Centerville Historical Society

Fulling mills were as essential as gristmills to the early colonists, for they "made full" or "felted" the material woven by the ladies on their home looms. There were at least five on Cape Cod and many more operating on streams in the two colonies. When commercial woolen mills were established, the fulling mills faded into oblivion, and other industries occupied their premises. Now only markers remain, like this one at Routes 149 and 28 in Marstons Mills. Photograph courtesy of the Barnstable Historical Commission

The Vodon shop became a laundry, then by 1930 a residence. Today it has been newly renovated by new owner Tom Ellis, a Channel Seven Boston newsman. Photograph courtesy of William Chase

In 1797 the General Court of Massachusetts required all towns to make an accurate survey of their academies, meetinghouses, courthouses, gristmills (water or wind), sawmills, paper mills, ironworks, iron ore, oil mills, fulling mills, card manufacturing, potash works, and waterfalls.

The result is the above map, which is a fascinating revelation of the location and composition of the natural resources and the industries of the growth era. Photograph by Dick Holbrook; courtesy of the Cape Cod Community College Library

Mills like this spread farther down the Cape. The Old East Mill at Heritage Plantation of Sandwich once stood on Snow's Hill in Orleans. Built in 1800, it ground corn, rye, and barley as well as salt from the Roberts Cove Salt Works. After several moves in Orleans, the mill was restored and moved to its present site in 1968. The mill still grinds corn in the summer for visitors to the seventy-six-acre museum of Americana. Photograph courtesy of the Heritage Plantation of Sandwich

Ye Ideal Pirate

Pirates have always been rumored to have buried treasure in Cape Cod sands. One of the most notorious pirates was Captain Samuel Bellamy of the Whidah (shown here), who was returning from a cruise in southern waters laden with loot when a storm descended in the spring of 1717. The ship was wrecked off Cahoon's Hollow in Wellfleet, and Bellamy and 144 pirates were drowned. Two survivors reached shore alive—Thomas Davis, a Welshman who had been impressed, and John Julian, a Cape Cod Indian.

The two alerted Samuel Harding of Wellfleet to the rich plunder, and all of them returned with horse and wagon to pick up treasure before anyone else knew of the wreck. Although the beach was soon crowded with carts and scavengers, Bellamy's chest of gold coins was never found. Photograph of painting from Truro, Cape Cod by Shebnah Rich; courtesy of the Cape Cod Community College Library

King George III found his national debt in 1765 to be rising uncontrollably. He and his advisors enacted the Stamp Act, which taxed legal documents, pamphlets, newspapers, licenses, ships papers, playing cards, and ballad broadsides. The reaction in America was immediate and violent. Etching from Songs of 76 by Max Brand; photograph from the Vuilleumier collection

Colonists denouncing the Stamp Act. Etching from Songs of 76 by Max Brand; photograph from the Vuilleumier collection

Thomas Hutchinson was governor of the Massachusetts Bay Colony from 1771-1774 when the tensions between Colony and Crown were reaching the conflagration point. The portrait was painted by Edward Truman and is from Portraits of Men 1670-1936, *issued by the Massachusetts Historical Society. Photograph courtesy of the Massachusetts Historical Society and the Cape Cod Community College Library*

Mural at the State House in Boston, Massachusetts, showing James Otis arguing against the Writs of Assistance before Governor Thomas Hutchinson and the justices. Photograph courtesy of the Bostonian Society

There were many confrontations between Loyalists and Patriots in the Colonies. Here a Loyalist has been tarred and feathered. The only recorded incident on Cape Cod is the tarring and feathering of "Widow Nabby" Mistress Abigail Freeman in Barnstable. Etching from Songs of 76 *by Max Brand; photograph from the Vuilleumier collection*

Mercy Otis Warren had turned to writing early. She poured out her first thoughts in poetry. When the conflict between England and the United Colonies became intense, she wrote satires against the British. These were published in Boston papers under a pen name, since it was deemed improper for women to be published. Her most lasting literary contribution was a three volume history of the American Revolution.

Mrs. James Warren (Mercy Otis) painted by John Singleton Copley (1738-1815); oil on canvas 51½x41 in. (130.1x104.1 cm.) painted about 1763; 31.212, Bequest of Winslow Warren; photograph of painting courtesy of the Museum of Fine Arts, Boston, Massachusetts

The Olde Colonial Courthouse, built in 1772, was the setting in 1774 for an enormous protest march. Over 1,500 people gathered on September 27 to stop the session of the King's court because Parliament had authorized sheriffs to appoint jurors rather then have their names drawn by selectmen.

This "Body of the People" march was one of the first organized protests against the British government in the colonies and a forerunner of the American Revolution. A liberty pole in the foreground is a replica of the original around which patriots gathered. The building became the Third Baptist Church when it was no longer needed as a courthouse. In recent years it has become the home of the Tales of Cape Cod, Inc. and features memorabilia of the Revolutionary period. *Photograph courtesy of the Barnstable Historical Commission*

This carved wooden statue of Justice once stood atop the 1772 Olde Colonial Courthouse in Barnstable Village. The statue is now on exhibit in the Shelburne Museum in Vermont. *Photograph courtesy of the Trayser Museum*

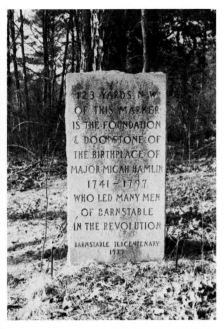

As soon as word was received from Lexington of the "dreadful encounter" of April 19, 1775, nineteen men were mustered from the militia and sent to help the colonists. Captain Micah Hamlin was in charge, as he also was later when his company was sent to help in the defense of Boston in 1776. Hamlin rose to the rank of major and was probably one of the most outstanding soldiers of the American Revolution. The marker stands on Route 149.

Others who commanded Cape Cod companies were Colonel Joseph Otis and Captain Nathaniel Freeman. Photograph courtesy of the Barnstable Historical Commission

During the American Revolution scarcely a day went by that enemy ships were not within gunshot of the coastline. Falmouth experienced the most traumatic time, however, when the town was bombarded for five-and-a-half hours on Saturday, April 3, 1779. Cannonball, double-headed shot, bars of iron and grape shot were flung into the village by ten British ships anchored in a row off Shore Street beach. Two schooners and eight sloops fired toward trenches where the militia was ready to repulse any landing party.

Major Joseph Dimmick walked the breastwork, according to the Falmouth Enterprise anniversary edition in 1976, "keeping his men from showing their heads and defying bullets from the enemy." There was much relief when the British ships sailed away without landing.

Artist Franklin Gifford pictured the event in this painting, which is now owned by the Falmouth Historical Society. Photograph by Dick Holbrook; courtesy of the Falmouth Historical Society

The Old Powder House on the grounds of Brooks Academy in Harwich Center is the only remaining authentic Revolutionary-period ammunition depot on Cape Cod. The tiny structure, topped with the carving of an American eagle, stood originally opposite Brooks Park, the training ground for the militia. From 1770 to 1784 it held powder, shot, and shells. It is the property of the Harwich Historical Society. Photograph by Pierre DuPont Vuilleumier

CAPE COD B

The Cape Cod Bicentennial Painting, by Falmouth artist Karen Rinaldo, was created in 1976 for the nation's 200th birthday. She also painted similar montages for each of the fifteen towns in Barnstable County. The original is part of the Falmouth Historical Society Collection.

It is a composite of scenes in the fifteen towns including "the United States the Paul Revere Bell, whaling ship, houses, the Barnstable court he churches, the Provincetown fishing

Pilgrim Monument, dunes, the Marconi
tion, the Brewster Mill, the cranberry
s and cranberry pickers, the Indian
eting House, the Sandwich Museum,
harbors, the ferry, the Woods Hole water-
front, the Bourne Bridge, the airport at
Hyannis, condominiums and the Kennedy
Memorial" (from Cape Cod/200, by
Rinaldo). Photograph by Hugo Poisson;
courtesy of the Falmouth Historical Society
and Karen Rinaldo

During the bicentennial year, the County Bicentennial Commission issued a bicentennial calendar to the media using the Liberty Cape symbol as a logo. This representative issue from the June 10 Caper magazine, gives the flavor of events of that significant year. Photograph courtesy of the All-Cape Bicentennial Commission

The Barnstable County Militia, reactivated for the bicentennial, drills in front of the Revolutionary-period Olde Colonial Courthouse. Falmouth's Militia Company was also reactivated for the festivities. Photograph by Pierre DuPont Vuilleumier

*F*ive political entities from the village to the nation were represented in Village of Flags Bicentennial parade in West Barnstable in September 1975. From left to right can be seen Mary Carlson, West Barnstable Village chairman; Marion Vuilleumier, secretary for the Town Commission; Louis Cataldo, Barnstable County coordinator; Patricia Harrington, Massachusetts Commission staff; and John Warner, who was then the administrator of the American Revolution Bicentennial Administration in Washington, D.C. and is now the senator from Virginia. Photograph by Stephen Gens; from Cape Cod Illustrated

On July 7, 1981, the Bicentennial Committee arranged for the burial of a time capsule on the grounds of the Town Hall. Bicentennial coordinator Louis Cataldo (left), Selectmen Gloria Rudman and Alfred Buckler (center back) watch as Frank A. Maki, Jr. of the Century Vault Company of West Barnstable and Stephen B. Williams of Cotuit (left) lower the 200-pound container into the ground.

Among the many items in the vault which is slated for opening in 2076, is a bank book with a $200 deposit. Based on today's interest rates, the account should have in it $63,000—enough for the Tri-centennial Committee to have a rousing celebration! Photograph by Fred Bodenseik; courtesy of the Barnstable Patriot

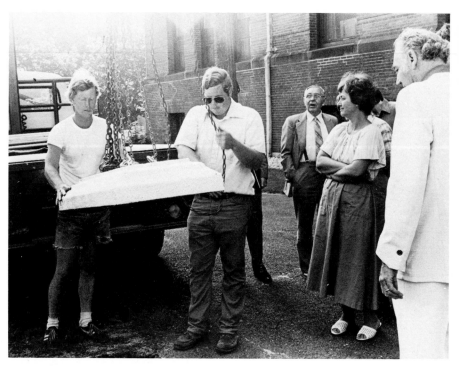

While wounds of war were healing the new country had to organize. Money had to be collected, and the quickest way was to tax shipping. The Customs House on Cobb's Hill in Barnstable was headquarters of the northside customs district for more than 100 years beginning in 1789. Domestic ships were registered, documented, and enrolled here, while foreign vessels were cleared here by customs officials. Also, cargoes were bonded, bounties were paid to fisherman, and other activities connected with maritime commerce took place in this historic brick structure.

When Barnstable was merged with the Boston Customs District in 1913, the building became a post office. Then in 1960, the building was given to the town by the federal government and became the Donald G. Trayser Memorial Museum. Named for the Barnstable newsman, historian, and author, the building now contains extensive memorabilia of Cape Cod. Photograph courtesy of the Barnstable Historical Commission

A new country also had to think of safeguarding its coast, so the beginnings of the Coast Guard (the Revenue Service) was established. Later this would join with Life Saving Service and the Lighthouse Service to become today's organization.

The Boston District, which includes Cape Cod, is pictured here with locations of lighthouses marked. Photograph of map by Steven LeClair; courtesy of the Cape Cod Community College Library

Another customs house was built in Woods Hole. In 1789 the United States formally established Custom District VII, which included all of the Cape except Falmouth, which was attached to Edgartown. Two years later the Falmouth customs was connected to Barnstable but remained a sub-port to Barnstable, along with Provincetown, Wellfleet, Sandwich, Hyannis, Chatham, and Dennis. Deputy collectors handled the collections and passed them on to the Barnstable District collector. Photograph courtesy of the Falmouth Historical Society

When smallpox claimed victims, the dead were buried in smallpox cemeteries. This small cemetery is in Hockanum Hills, Yarmouth, and dates to 1796. Photograph courtesy of the Historical Society of Old Yarmouth

Samplers were a favorite way of expressing feelings as this Shiverick mourning sampler shows. Photograph courtesy of the Falmouth Historical Society

Highland Light (or Cape Cod Light) in Truro was the Cape's first lighthouse, with its initial version built in 1797. Isaac Small, the keeper, was kept busy filling, trimming, and lighting twenty-four whale oil lamps. Rebuilt in 1857 and electrified in 1932, the 1,000-watt bulb, magnified by bull's-eye lenses, shines twenty miles out to sea. Photograph courtesy of the Cape Cod Chamber of Commerce

Known as the twin sisters of Chatham, these lighthouses were erected about 1800. In the early days, lighthouses were known by their number of lights rather than by the timing of their blinks, so, seeing these twins, seamen would stand off the dangerous shoals. Photograph courtesy of Robert Severy

Tarpaulin Cove on Naushon Island was a haven for many ships, but occasionally a severe storm dashed one to bits. Here the ship Perseverance is shown being wrecked January 31, 1805, as its crew escapes safely to shore. The painting is by Corne, and the original is in the Peabody Museum of Salem. Photograph from Early History of Naushon Island by Amelia Forbes Emerson; courtesy of the trustees of the Naushon Island Trust and the Cape Cod Community College Library

John "Mad Jack" Percival, born in West Barnstable, went to sea in his early teens as a cabin boy and cook. After many adventures at sea, he joined the United States Navy in 1809. He became a captain during the War of 1812. Percival earned his nickname by a wild gamble when, in order to celebrate July 4, 1813, he captured the British ship the Beagle, which was blockading New York Harbor. United States Navy photograph

The U.S.S. Constitution "Old Ironsides," the country's oldest warship, is pictured here by artist B. Snyder of Vermont. The ship sailed around the world in 1844-1846 with Mad Jack as her commander.

Prior to this command he led his crew of the sloop Peacock to victory over the British frigate Epervier during the War of 1812. He was known as a superb seaman and an inspiring leader. Percival spent his last years in Dorchester but was buried in the West Barnstable cemetery. Painting from the Vuilleumier collection

Falmouth was fired upon in January 1814. The British brig Nimrod fired cannonballs for several hours but did not try to land. Artist Lloyd Nightingale pictured the event in this drawing. Photograph courtesy of the Falmouth Historical Society

This rare document is a pass to Silas Bourne and his schooner Minerva of Falmouth, signed November 13, 1809, by James Madison, president of the United States. It allowed Bourne to move merchandise without hindrance up and down the coast. Note the curvy top which is made to fit a companion pass to show the document was genuine. The embargo was causing havoc to shipping, and passes such as this were needed. Photograph by Dick Holbrook; courtesy of the Bourne Town Archives

The only other town to skirmish with the British in the War of 1812 was Orleans. When Captain Richard Raggot of the British ship Spencer said he would destroy the saltworks if he did not receive $1,000, the request was immediately denied. When the red coated troops landed on December 19, 1814, they were met with resistance by the local militia and were turned back.

In this reenactment in November 1975, the British troops were portrayed by the fourth Battalion Company of Massachusetts, Sixty-Fourth regiment of Foot from the Greater New Bedford area. The Cape Cod Barnstable County Militia portrayed their counterparts of long ago. Photograph by Pierre DuPont Vuilleumier

In spite of the uncertainties of war, business at home had to continue. One sign of confidence in the fledgling country was the start of a bank. The Falmouth National Bank (at left) is pictured in its first home on Main Street. Established in 1821, it is the Cape's oldest. The original capital stock was $100,000. Photograph from Saconesset by Theodate Geoffrey; courtesy of the Falmouth Historical Society

In 1821 Elijah Swift, with Ward Parker and Thomas Swift, was the founder of the Falmouth National Bank. He became its first president. In 1832 Swift planted the elms around the green, many of which are so majestic today. Swift made his money in whaling and lumbering. Two of his whalers were the Awashonks and Uncas. The picture is from a lithograph by A. Trochster. Photograph courtesy of the Falmouth Historical Society

People were sure the economy of the sea would return, so shipbuilding continued. Here forty oxen are shown pulling the Status Ante Bellum to its launching in Falmouth in 1815. The painting is Franklin Lewis Gifford's rendering of the event. Gifford painted many Falmouth scenes in the early 1900s. Photograph by Dick Holbrook; courtesy of the Falmouth Historical Society

Since travel by water had become more hazardous during the two wars, land travel began in earnest. Stagecoaches became familiar sights on Cape roads. Stagecoach lines began regular runs after the Revolution.

William Hewin's mail stage, pictured here, ran from 1849 to 1873. It was one of the last lines to run regularly and ceased only when the railroad arrived and could provide better service. Photograph courtesy of th Falmouth Historical Society

The figurehead of the ship Imperial sailed for twenty-five years in the Atlantic, Pacific and Indian oceans as well as the China Sea and the Bay of Bengal. The captain was James Edward Crosby of Brewster. When the ship was converted into a coal barge in 1895, the figurehead was placed on a Brewster beach. Photograph from the Donald Doane Memorial Collection; courtesy of Tales of Cape Cod, Inc.

Chapter 5

Prosperity

1820-1860

Four decades of prosperity, unmatched in previous times, followed. The population more than doubled—from 15,000 in 1775 to 35,900 in 1860.

Men returned to the sea. Shipbuilding began in earnest, with small yards appearing in the towns of Harwich, Chatham, Truro, Barnstable, Bourne, and Provincetown.

It was East Dennis, though, that produced the breathtakingly beautiful vessels. There in the Shiverick shipyards were constructed those graceful clippers, some of the finest sailing ships ever launched. The *Wild Hunter*, *Belle of the West*, *Webfoot*, and *Hippogriffe* were four of these amazing ships which served the China trade, sailed the California coast, and continuously made record runs. These vessels brought wealth to Cape Codders and did much for the nation's prestige.

Whaling also brought fortunes to Cape Codders. When drift whales ceased to be found along the shores, men from the northeastern shores put out to sea to find these leviathans. Barnstable County men took an early lead in the trade. Their techniques were so good that some were called to Nantucket to teach the art. Between wars, whale men and whale ship owners brought prosperity to a devastated economy. In fact, many were more familiar with exotic spots of the world than with their own land.

Daniel Webster wrote to Dennis friends in 1851: "Gentlemen the nature of your population is somewhat peculiar. I have often been struck by the very great number of sea captains as well as other mariners, which the county of Barnstable and the neighboring Islands furnish. On the Cape and on the Islands, I have frequently conversed with persons who seemed as well acquainted with the Galapagos Islands, the Sandwich Islands, and some parts of New Holland, as with our counties of Hampshire and Berkshire."

Though the leadership in the whaling industry gradually passed to New Bedford and Nantucket, many noted whale men in the 1800s were Cape Cod natives. Like the skippers of the clipper ships, these captains created worldwide respect for the Stars and Stripes. In effect, these sea captains often performed services for the government, and thus were the forerunners of today's foreign diplomats.

The explosion of activity in the world of sail brought another of the Cape's familiar sights—the lighthouses. Highland Light, the first to direct its powerful beam to ships at sea, had been built on the vast clay cliffs at Truro in 1797. Most of the others were erected between 1816 and 1849. The associated, heroic Life-Saving Service that developed was to add another dimension to the oft-told tales of Cape Cod.

The Boston Sandwich Glass Company lighted its fires in Sandwich in 1824 and began producing its jewel-like wares. Deming Jarvis established the large factory with its cone-shaped chimneys that eventually employed over 500 workers and ran shifts around the clock. Experts in the art of glassblowing were imported from Europe, with their reputed strong backs, fireproof skins, and lungs of leather. Soon pressed and molded glass were being produced along with the blown, and the unusual products were shipped worldwide.

The Keith Car Works in Sagamore began in this era. Isaac Keith, in partnership with a blacksmith, began manufacturing carriages in 1846

Model of the packet Mail *on loan to the museum by Mrs. Alexander Crane of Barnstable. The* Mail, *skippered by Matthias Hinckley and Thomas Percival, was commissioned in 1837 and made regular runs to Boston from Barnstable with mail, freight, and passengers. It was a competitor of the* Commodore Hull *out of Yarmouth.*

On one exciting day the sloops raced to Boston in four-and-a-half hours, arriving practically neck and neck. Though the Mail *was said to have arrived three lengths ahead of her rival, "who won really depended on which side of the Barnstable/Yarmouth line you lived," according to the information card by the model. Photograph by Dick Holbrook; courtesy of the Trayser Museum*

Ships' figureheads were many and varied on the whalers, schooners, and clippers that sailed the seven seas. This beautifully preserved dapper gentleman once graced the prow of an early sailing vessel. Photograph courtesy of the Massachusetts Department of Commerce

under the name of Keith and Ryder. Carts, wagons, sleighs, and wheelbarrows were soon followed by stagecoaches and prairie schooners. When the railroad arrived in Sandwich in 1848, the company (renamed the Keith Manufacturing Company) found a ready market for freight cars. The business continued well into the next century, employing about 1,200 people and occupying an immense, sprawling, mile-long plant.

One of the high points of this century was the advance of the "iron horse" down the Cape. In 1854 the first train entering Hyannis was greeted by cheering crowds, cannon salutes, a band concert, and a clambake! The line pushed on to Orleans in 1865 and to Provincetown in 1873. The last spur, to Chatham, was laid in 1887.

Now the lowly cranberry, which from the beginning had been part of the Cape's food supply, came into prominence. The tart red fruit had long been a staple of the native Americans, who mixed the berries with deer meat to make *sassamanesh*. Pilgrims enjoyed its tang. In 1677 colonists had sent ten barrels to King Charles of England. Settlers ate the berries fresh and dried them for winter use. But when Henry Hall of Dennis began the first bogs, neighbors joined in the cultivation and the industry was born.

Another industry occupied Cape men, particularly in the town of Bourne. Deposits of iron ore made possible the manufacture of farm tools and kitchen implements and pots. When these needs were satisfied, colonists turned to making nails, which were eventually traded around the globe. At the industry's height, eleven or twelve vessels could be counted at town wharves discharging ore and loading iron products. The Parker Mills, established in Wareham in 1819, continues as Tremont Nail Company to this day.

While these industries were flourishing, an earlier occupation was declining. Salt making had begun in Dennis in 1776 when Captain John Sears tried making it by evaporation. The fishermen needed large quantities to preserve their fish, and imported salt was expensive because of the taxes. In addition, the British blockade had driven the price higher. A bounty of three shillings per bushel had brought a burst of activity, and saltworks sprang up along the Cape shores. By 1802 there were 136 salt makers. During the War of 1812 the number jumped to 442. In the 1830s, $2 million was invested in salt making, and the return was 25 percent. The decline came in the 1840s, when mined salt became available and the railroads that began pushing insistently down the Cape could transport salt cheaply. Gradually the old saltworks were dismantled. The historian Simeon Deyo notes that the industry became extinct in 1888 when the arms of the last salt mills ceased on the Bass River shore.

Billingsgate Light in Wellfleet stood for many years on Billingsgate Point, a spot where the Pilgrims under Myles Standish landed on their first explorations from Provincetown. Erected in 1822, the lighthouse had thirty homes and a school as companions. It became evident that the land was washing away, so the light was moved back in 1868. Keeper Ingals reported further danger in 1889, and it was abandoned soon after. Today this land is completely submerged most of the time and is known as Billingsgate Shoal. Photograph from A Trip Around Cape Cod by E. G. Perry; courtesy of the Trayser Museum

Model of the ship Belle of the West, loaned by George Walsh. Sometimes referred to as "the finest ship ever built on Cape Cod," this graceful clipper was designed by Samuel Pooke and built in 1853 by the Shiverick brothers at Quivet Creek in East Dennis. Captain William Frederick Howes was her skipper for owner Christopher Hall until the Belle was sold to Eastern owners and foundered in the Bay of Bengal in 1868. Photograph by Dick Holbrook; courtesy of the Trayser Museum

Many a ship was outfitted at the old Sail Loft in Hyannis. Josiah H. Hallett was sail maker. Photograph courtesy of the Trayser Museum

The steamer Pilgrim was one of several which carried passengers between New York and Fall River, where trains waited to carry them to Boston and Cape Cod. These steamers were part of the Old Colony Railroad system. Photograph from the History of the Old Colony Railroad, edited and published by Louis Hager and Albert Handy; courtesy of the Cape Cod Community College Library

The interiors of the Old Colony Line steamers were grand affairs as this view shows. Photograph from the History of the Old Colony Railroad, edited and published by Louis Hager and Albert Handy; courtesy of the Cape Cod Community College Library

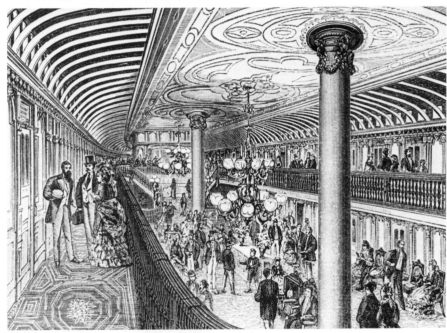

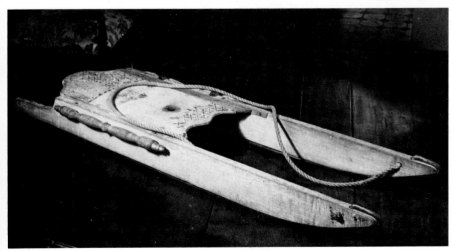

This beautifully decorated child's sled had a hole in the center so it could be made into a "bob sled." There is much evidence that toys and games of this period were fashioned with great care for the youngsters. This sled probably dates to the early 1800s. Photograph by Dick Holbrook; courtesy of the Trayser Museum

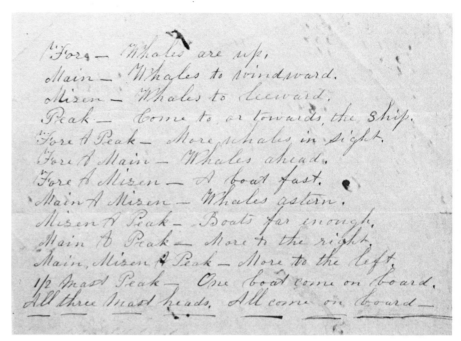

Fore. — *Whales are up.*
Main — *Whales to windward.*
Mizen — *Whales to leeward.*
Peak — *Come to, or towards, the ship.*
Fore & Peak — *More whales in sight.*
Fore & Main — *Whales ahead.*
Fore & Mizen — *A boat fast.*
Main & Mizen — *Whales astern.*
Mizen & Peak — *Boats far enough.*
Main & Peak — *More to the right.*
Main, Mizen & Peak — *More to the left.*
1/2 Mast Peak — *One boat come on board.*
All three Mast heads, All come on board —

Secret whaling signals of the ship Addison, *Samuel Lawrence, master, of New Bedford, 1856-1860. The handwriting is of Mary Chipman Lawrence, his wife, who together with their five-year-old daughter, Minnie, accompanied the captain on the Pacific Ocean voyage.*

These signals were used to direct the whaleboats toward the location of the whales as seen from the masthead of the parent ship. These signals were kept secret because of the fierce competition among the ships. Photograph by Dick Holbrook; courtesy of the Falmouth Historical Society

Whaling was an economic mainstay, and many a Cape Cod man visited the Seaman's Bethel in New Bedford before embarking on a whaling voyage. Standing on Johnny Cake Hill next to the Whaling Museum, this tiny church, dedicated in 1832, was referred to by Herman Melville in Moby Dick as the "Whaleman's Chapel." "Few are the moody fishermen, shortly bound for the Indian or Pacific Oceans who failed to make a Sunday visit to this spot." Inside are twenty-three cenotaphs memorializing sailors lost at sea, some as late as 1934.

This port peaked as a whaling center in 1857 with 329 whale ships, while 95 more sailed from neighboring towns. Many Cape Codders formed the crews and captained the whaling vessels. Photograph by Nicholas Whitman; courtesy of the Whaling Museum, New Bedford

Harpooning a whale. Photograph of engraving courtesy of the Cape Cod Community College Library

Towing the dead whale to the mother ship was a hefty task. Photograph of engraving courtesy of the Cape Cod Community College Library

Lifting the carcass of the whale aboard, where it would be cut into strips, melted into oil on deck "try-works," then put in barrels for the long trip home. Photograph of engraving courtesy of the Cape Cod Community College Library

There were many hours when sailors were idle, waiting for a whale to "blow," and some of these were spent in creating scrimshaw from whale's teeth. This decorated tooth from the ship Decatur is an excellent example. The Decatur sailed from New Bedford in 1818. Photograph from The Yankee Scrimshanders by Fredrika Burrows; courtesy of Mrs. Burrows

Cleaning the whalebone on a whale ship. Photograph courtesy of the Falmouth Historical Society

The old whaler's store in Falmouth was a center for visiting as well as for purchasing in the mid-1800s. Photograph courtesy of the Falmouth Historical Society

Bass River Upper Bridge, which connected South Dennis with South Yarmouth, was the first of three bridges to traverse the river since 1833. The toll house, abutting the bridge in the center of the picture, was built in 1833. Here tolls were collected from all passersby except ministers and funeral processions. There were originally shareholders, mostly from South Dennis, who held stock in this first bridge.

In the background are homesteads fronting on Main Street, South Dennis, a sea captains' village where names like Baker, Downs, Crowell, Bangs, Kelley, Nickerson, and Underwood have been familiar names for generations. Photograph from the Edmond Rhodes Nickerson Collection of South Dennis

Liberty Hall, South Dennis, is pictured in 1913 when it was the location of Jethro Baker's Furniture Ware Room. (Note mattress at front door.) The building was believed to have been moved to its present site in 1844 by owners Weston Baker and Isaac Downs.

Through the years the building has served as a dry and fancy goods store, doctor's office, millinery store, stove showroom, post office, stagecoach stop, ice cream parlor, as well as a center for social events in the village. In 1920 Ella Stephenson Totten gave the building and adjoining land to the inhabitants of the village of South Dennis, and until 1943 it was called Totten Hall. Since then it has been the site of village suppers, plays, socials, a summertime thrift shop, and a meeting place for many groups. Photograph from the Edmond Rhodes Nickerson Collection of South Dennis

Johnson Hall stands on the grounds of the Yarmouth Camp Grounds Association where Methodist camp meetings were held from 1863 to 1945. Built about 1890, the hall honors a prominent preacher of that era, Reverend Oscar E. Johnson.

Camp meetings were held originally in Wellfleet in 1819, then in Eastham at Millenium Grove from 1828 to 1862. A grove on Willow Street on the Yarmouth/Barnstable line was purchased and the camp meetings held there in a large tabernacle no longer standing. Tiny gingerbread or carpenter Gothic-style homes still cluster together in neighborly fashion though gatherings are more social. Several times a year services are held in the hall with clergy residents preaching. Photograph courtesy of Irving Lovell

The Barnstable Academy, founded in 1839 and shown from an old daguerreotype of 1850, was one of the earliest public schools of higher education on the Cape. The building is now attached to the Bacon Farm in Barnstable.

The earliest private school of higher learning was in Sandwich. It was incorporated by the state legislature in 1804. The site, near the Hoxie House, is marked with a bronze plaque set in stone. Photograph courtesy of the Trayser Museum

The Old Salt Works in South Yarmouth on Bass River showing the drying vats and the roofs that covered them in rainy weather. These were the last of the salt making establishments, which by 1802 were producing over 40,000 bushels of salt and 182,000 bushels of Glauber salt (a medicinal product). Photograph courtesy of the Historical Society of Old Yarmouth

Cranberry picking time in one of the Cape's many bogs. When the cranberry harvest was ready, school was cancelled to free all hands to pick the tangy red berries. One of the best cranberry years was 1895 when 150,000 barrels worth $1 million were harvested. Cultivation began in 1816 and continues to this day. Photographs courtesy of the Historical Society of Old Yarmouth

WILLIAM D. HOLMES,
Manufacturer and Dealer in
Fine Hand-Made Harnesses
BARNSTABLE, MASS.

Harness making was a fine business in the mid-1800s, as this advertisement of William Holmes of Hyannis shows. Photograph courtesy of John Howland Crocker

The Pocasset Iron Company was founded as a blast furnace in 1822 by Hercules Weston. In 1852 it was sold and became the iron works. The plant was situated on the banks of Barlow's River and was the oldest industry in the village. It continued operation for over sixty years in spite of being burnt out twice and rebuilt. Photograph courtesy of Bourne Town Archives

These three decorative iron plaques, about twelve inches square, were made at the Pocasset Iron Company. Photographs courtesy of Helen M. Watt

These chimneys of the Boston and Sandwich Glass Company kept a constant pall of smoke over Sandwich for sixty-three years. The buildings, with their fiery furnaces which consumed over 2,000 acres of forests, have now been demolished. The jewel-like products produced here are on display in the Sandwich Historical Society's Glass Museum. The plant was eventually closed because of a dispute and ensuing strike over a worker's wage. Photograph courtesy of Tales of Cape Cod, Inc.

This hanging candle lamp has a hexagonal tin frame with tooled decoration. Six alternating cobalt blue and ruby cut overlay panels surround the lamp. The central panel is engraved with a design of the Bunker Hill Monument. It was made by the Boston and Sandwich Glass Company probably about the time of the completion of the monument in 1843. Photograph by W. Gordon Swan; courtesy of the Sandwich Historical Society

The "Lafayet" boat salt made by the Boston and Sandwich Glass Company is the only piece of pressed glass marked in the mold with the factory's name. The stern is marked "B. & S. Glass Co." Photograph by W. Gordon Swan; courtesy of the Sandwich Historical Society

This small covered jar was blown at the Boston and Sandwich Glass factory in 1859 for the tenth wedding anniversary of Melinda Nye Fish Chipman and Isaac Kimball Chipman. The jar, which has a very tight stopper, still contains cookies made by Melinda for her husband Isaac, who was head carpenter at the Boston and Sandwich Glass Company. Photograph by W. Gordon Swan; courtesy of the Sandwich Historical Society

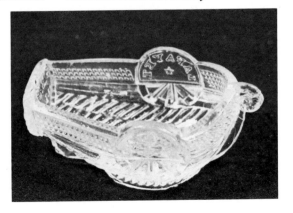

Dolls have always been popular. This Joel Ellis doll, patented about 1873, has been enjoyed by many children. Photograph from the Fredrika Burrows collection

Keith Car and Manufacturing Company of Sagamore was one of the largest employers on Cape Cod in the early part of this century. Photograph courtesy of the Bourne Town Archives

Many of these prairie schooners were built by I. N. Keith for the California gold rush in 1849. From the booklet Cape Cod, published by the Bourne Historical Society in 1926; courtesy of the Bourne Town Archives

Wagons, ox carts, and sleighs like these were produced by Isaac Keith and his partner Mr. Ryder, who was a blacksmith, in the early 1800s. By 1848, when the railroad reached the town of Sandwich, the company began building freight cars. One of the earliest cars was a small one for carrying sand or coal designed by Keith. Sons Hiram and Isaac worked with their father and by 1869 took over the business. Isaac's son Eben brought the business into the twentieth century. It eventually became a subsidiary of the Standard Steel Company of Pittsburgh, Pennsylvania.

Eben entered politics in 1906, when he was elected a state senator. He was later a member of the Governor's Council and was several times a delegate to Republican national conventions. Photographs courtesy of Tales of Cape Cod, Inc.

By 1865 the railroad had chugged as far as Orleans, so Brewster had its railroad station. Like most of the Cape Cod depots, this was of simple design, in contrast to its elaborate Chatham neighbor. Photograph courtesy of Tales of Cape Cod, Inc.

The old Chatham Railroad station near the end of Depot Street was in use from 1887 to 1937. Gingerbread decorations are a reminder of the Victorian era. Though the town was the last to be reached by the railroad, it is the one with the finest reminder of those days. The building is now a museum containing models, documents, photos, and other memorabilia of railroading days. Photograph courtesy of Tales of Cape Cod, Inc.

When the railroad reached Provincetown, it found streets of sand but sidewalks of boards. Residents found it difficult to trudge through the sand on their daily errands. They left that chore mostly to the horses. Photograph from the History of the Old Colony Railroad, edited and published by Louis Hager and Albert Handy; courtesy of the Cape Cod Community College Library

Among the outstanding citizens who lived in this period was Chief Justice Lemuel Shaw of Barnstable. He served as head of the Massachusetts Supreme Court from 1830 to 1860. Photograph from a painting by William Morris Hunt; courtesy of the Trayser Museum

Daniel Webster, lawyer, senator, and secretary of state, was a frequent visitor to Sandwich between 1815 and 1851. He favored the fishing and had a special room reserved for him at the Fessenden Tavern in Sandwich.

Webster took credit for persuading Lemuel Shaw of Barnstable to accept appointment as chief justice of the Massachusetts Supreme Court. Photograph from Historic Pilgrimages in New England by Edwin N. Bacon; courtesy of the Trayser Museum

Mrs. Francis E. Swift of Falmouth for many years wrote for current magazines and newspapers under the pen name Fanny Fales. In 1853 she published Voices of the Heart. She was known as an "easy and graceful versifier." Photograph courtesy of the Falmouth Historical Society

Reverend Joseph "Blind Joe" Amos, pastor and tribal official, brought the Baptist denomination to Mashpee. Though blind since childhood, he was a gifted speaker and leader. He was ordained by the American Baptists in 1830 at the age of twenty-five. Photograph courtesy of the Mashpee Baptist Church

Nathan Henry Chamberlayne, Unitarian minister born in Monument Beach in 1828, was another of the Cape's first authors. He is pictured here with his dog Foxy after his retirement in 1889 to Bourne. His Autobiography of a New England Farmhouse, *published in 1884, is a novel but is based on his upbringing in the Sandwich poorhouse operated by his father. He wrote many articles, sermons, tracts, and at least three major books. Photograph from the Bourne Historical Society Collection; courtesy of the Bourne Town Archives*

There are records of midgets on the Cape and the Islands a century ago, perhaps because there were fewer people and more intermarriage. These are the Adams sisters of Martha's Vineyard who entertained on the Keith's circuit. Ruth Washburn, who grew up in the Falmouth Congregational Parsonage, recalls visiting at the home of Miss Lydia Robinson, who often entertained the famous sisters when they awaited a conveyance to take them to the Woods Hole boat for the Vineyard:

> *They were dainty midgets who had appeared with Tom Thumb, the midget of Barnum and Bailey fame. These little women were alert of mind and vivacious. . . . What an experience it was to see them climb into a chair, turn about as a small child is wont to do and finally settle back feet straight out. . . . In their wee hands a teaspoon resembled a shovel. They wore tiny bonnets and capes, as was the fashion for all women of that day. When they left in the stage for Woods Hole, it was as if we were losing our dolls.*

Photograph courtesy of the Falmouth Historical Society

At this political parade in front of the Falmouth Hotel, the placard for governor hopeful William Nye was carried by a midget. He was about the height of a wagon wheel in this last century photograph.

It could have been one of the "seven little Hatches of Falmouth," as described by Ruth Hale-Hatch in the Hatch Genealogy.

When Barnabas Hatch married Abigail Swift "it is said he married a near relative which accounted for the fact that seven of his nine children were so small. They were under four feet in height and four of them were so low in stature as to stand under a common door latch, but they lived to be quite aged and well educated and much respected." According to a supporting diagram, the midgets were Hannah, Anna, Rebecca, Barnabas, Robinson, Jesse, and Nabby. Photograph courtesy of the Falmouth Historical Society

Looking out of the upper window is Woodrow "Woody" Hinckley of Barnstable, one of the Cape's "little people" or midgets. Woody was self-conscious about his lack of height, so when his class was pictured in 1864 in Barnstable Village's school (now the Thrift Shop and Service Center of the Cape Cod Council of Churches) Woody chose a high perch.

For many years Woody was postmaster for the village of Barnstable, and he placed the post office boxes low enough to suit himself. There is no record of any patron grumbling. Woody's brother Oliver was also a midget.

Another respected midget was Isaiah Hatch of South Wellfleet, who at his death at the age of fifty-two was three feet, seven inches tall and weighed eighty pounds. Photograph courtesy of John Howland Crocker

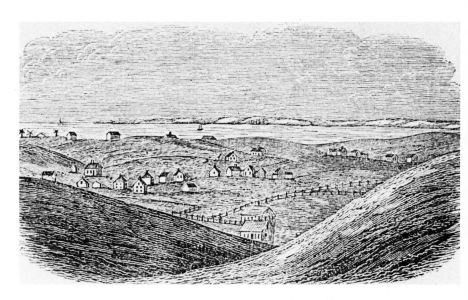

The town of Chatham as it looked prior to 1839, according to John Warner Barber, who gathered "a general collection of interesting facts, traditions, biographical sketches, anecdotes, etc., relating to the history and antiquities of every town of Massachusetts, with geographical descriptions." Photograph courtesy of the Cape Cod Community College Library

Villages began to have a permanent look, as seen in this eastern view of Pond Village, Truro, pictured before 1839 by an engraving from John Warner Barber's History and Antiquities of Every Town in Massachusetts. *Photograph of engraving courtesy of the Cape Cod Community College Library*

This northern view of Wellfleet Harbor taken from an engraving before 1839 shows ships, windmills, and not a very large settlement. Photograph courtesy of the Cape Cod Community College Library

The town of Brewster as it looked prior to 1839, according to John Warner Barber's History and Antiquities of Every Town in Massachusetts, which was illustrated by 200 engravings. Photograph courtesy of the Cape Cod Community College Library

Robert Claybrook of South Carolina, an emancipated slave, came North and lived in Bournedale, near Herring Pond. He is pictured here about 1908. Photograph courtesy of the Bourne Town Archives

Chapter 6

Civil War

1861-1865

In the 1850s, Abolitionists began to surface in Cape Cod towns. "Come-Outers" withdrew from churches and organizations that they felt countenanced slavery. Enterprising seamen used their vessels to bring slaves North for their furtive trips on the Underground Railroad, where runaways were passed from home to home until they reached freedom. When Fort Sumter was fired upon in April 1861, local folk united for the coming struggle. There was more unanimity in this war than in any previous one, though it too interrupted the Cape's development.

On May 8, 1861, three weeks after President Abraham Lincoln called for volunteers, an enthusiastic company called the Sandwich Guards marched to Boston, fourth volunteer company in the state. Yarmouth's Joseph Hamlin was the Cape's most distinguished Civil War army officer, eventually attaining the rank of Brevet Major General. Since the sea was a natural theater for Cape men, many were in the navy and on privateers.

When Lee surrendered to Grant at Appomattox on April 9, 1865, the cessation of hostilities was a blessed relief to a torn and bankrupt nation. There was rejoicing, however, that the Union was preserved and that freedom had been established as the basis for the society.

Now, many residents thought, the Cape could rebuild its shattered economy and move into the coming decades with new hope.

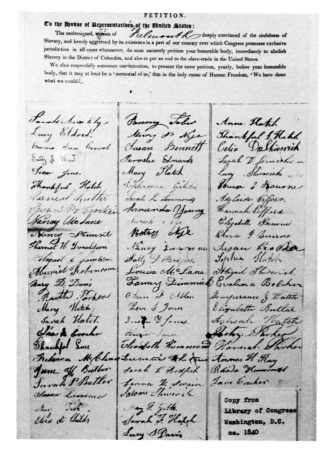

Deming Jarves, later the founder of the Boston and Sandwich Glass Company, is pictured in his uniform as second lieutenant of the Twenty-Fourth Massachusetts Infantry. At age twenty-three he was the acting signal officer of a field telegraph train at the headquarters of the Army of the Cumberland. The photo was taken in September of 1863, upon his departure from a hospital in Nashville. He was "down to 125 pounds from his usual 155." Photograph courtesy of the Trayser Museum

Falmouth women were against slavery, as this petition to the House of Representatives in 1840 indicates.

Cape Codders were generally united against slavery, and abolitionists had been active for two decades preceding the Civil War. More than one shipmaster had brought runaway blacks North to freedom. Others, like Captain George Lovell of Osterville, landed slaves on the Cape's south shore and used an underground railroad across the Cape to the bay, where they were assisted farther north. Photograph courtesy of the Falmouth Historical Society

Yours truly
M. E. Hamblin

Joseph Eldridge Hamblin, a native of Yarmouth, was the only field officer on the Cape to attain the rank of brevet major-general during the Civil War. Hamblin's biography was prepared by Deborah Hamblin "from scanty information, with valuable aid from Mrs. Thomas Bray," using material from the Historical Branch of the Yarmouth Public Library. A descendant, Deborah Hamblin noted in the 1902 booklet, "The present generation cannot realize the spirit of those days in the early sixties." Photography from the booklet Brevet Major-General Hamblin by Deborah Hamblin; courtesy of the Cape Cod Community College Library

John J. Ryder of West Brewster was the first man from Brewster to enlist when President Abraham Lincoln called for volunteers in 1862. The first battle he fought in was Chancellorsville. He was in the Lookout Mountain and Gettysburg battles and marched with General Sherman to the sea. Wounded in the battle of Kenesaw Mountain, he was invalided home for the rest of the war. Photograph courtesy of the Cape Cod Community College Library

John J. Ryder wrote Reminiscences of Three Years' Service in the Civil War. It was published in 1928, when he was one of the very few survivors of the Civil War veterans. In succeeding years no military parade was complete without Ryder dressed as Uncle Sam. He had moved to Buzzards Bay in 1871 and was commander of E. B. Nye Post No. 203 in Bourne. Photograph from the Donald Doane Memorial Collection; courtesy of Tales of Cape Cod, Inc.

FOURTH OF JULY 1880.

To Commissioned Officers, Enlisted Men, and Volunteers of the Barnstable White Horse Cavalry, Attention!

You are ordered to meet at Masonic Hall, Barnstable, Wednesday Evening, June 30th, to make arrangements for the proper celebration of the 4th of July. The meeting will be called to order at 7.30 o'clock, sharp.

Division Officers stationed at West Barnstable, Yarmouthport, and Centreville are directed to give due notice to their respective commands and send delegates to a general meeting to be called some time during the week.

Look sharp for subsequent orders.

PER ORDER COMMANDER.

Five cavalry regiments with over 300 men served in the Civil War, according to Simeon Deyo's history. Though none was officially named the "White Horse Cavalry," no doubt this call to gather and celebrate the Fourth of July, 1880, was for those who survived their activity in the Grand Army of the Republic. Photograph courtesy of John Howland Crocker

Thomas Warren Jones, who died in November 1927 at age eighty-three, was one of the Cape's last surviving heroes of the Civil War. Jones enlisted at age fifteen. He was in several of the most severe engagements, ranging from the battles of Bull Run to Gettysburg. He was wounded in battle and carried evidence of this throughout his life. Jones was a stonemason and worked on the county courthouse and the Episcopal church, St. Andrews-By-The-Sea in Hyannis Port. Photograph courtesy of Patricia Anderson

Battery B Fourth United States Light Artillery gathered in Hyannis September 9, 1893. Photograph courtesy of the Cape Cod Community College Library

Nobska Lighthouse first shone its beacon over Nantucket Sound in 1828. By 1878 the government had built a new tall steel lighthouse. On top was a fixed white light with a red section, warning sailors of dangerous shoals. Nobska Lighthouse, which still stands guard over the harbor, is the only Cape lighthouse with rocks at its base. Photograph copyright Julius Lazarus, Hyannis, Massachusetts

Chapter 7

Transition

1866-1871

In spite of high hopes following the Civil War, the economy refused to recover. A workers' strike at the Sandwich Glass Company, along with cheaper manufacturing practices in other areas, left glassblowers no occupation. Factories mushrooming near swift rivers in New England and the South took away the demand for the local cloth products. The coming of the age of steam idled seamen who were familiar only with the operation of sailing vessels.

Doldrums descended upon the villages. Though cranberrying, fishing, and farming yielded seasonal incomes, most people found the living meager. Young men sought their livelihood in banking, business, and manufacturing, which often took them off the Cape. Population on the peninsula declined from the pre-Civil War number of 35,900 at the rate of 105 persons yearly. By the turn of the century, there were only 27,000 inhabitants.

Ironically, though some of the major occupations had ceased, others were lying dormant, for Cape Codders had not yet realized what riches were all around them. There still remained the wonders of nature, which even the very earliest comers had noted. There was the infinite blue of the sky, the rosy-hued sunsets, golden beaches, and the azure ocean. But as one farmer mournfully enjoined when a visitor commented on the view, "Yes, but you can't eat it."

Town fathers, oblivious to the descending wave of tourists which would provide much eating money in the future, sought mainly for new industries to replace the old. In desperation a committee was formed to investigate making insulation from the enormous amount of seaweed washed up on the beaches.

While the economy dipped, culture gained a foothold. The Falmouth Social Library had begun a literary movement in 1792, followed shortly after in 1796 by Cotuit-Santuit residents who boasted the "second library of Cape Cod." In 1865 fourteen women met in the parlor of Mrs. Sylvester Baxter to form the Hyannis Literary Association, forerunner of the Hyannis Public Library. Eventually fifty libraries would develop from these small beginnings, not counting those in the public schools.

Lyceums, which proposed to "improve members in useful knowledge and advance popular education" were organized in many towns. Sometimes these Lyceum programs were held in special buildings like Lyceum Hall in Yarmouthport. In other towns these debates, lectures, concerts, and poetry readings were held in Liberty Halls or in churches.

Lyceum committees worked with schools, and debating was especially encouraged. Subjects ranged widely as in Yarmouth, where members were lectured on "The Genius and Poetry of Lord Byron" and received "sterling comments on fish" by Nat Atwood. Lyceums were forerunners of the many historical societies which later spread throughout the towns.

In May 1866 vessels were counted by the staff of the Nobska Lighthouse in Woods Hole. Careful records of all passing ships were kept by the lighthouse keepers. Many passed Nobska because it was on the inland passage from Boston to New York. This log accounts for maritime activity for several years. Photograph by Dick Holbrook; courtesy of the Falmouth Historical Society

Lifesaving along the New England coast was begun in 1786 by the Massachusetts Humane Society and supported by donations from the public. Shelter huts were built where stranded seamen could find food and relief from the cold. In 1871 Congress passed a bill organizing the United States Life Saving Service. Surf men and station keepers were hired to rescue stricken vessels and crews. Eventually the Cape had thirteen stations from the elbow at Chatham to the tip at Provincetown.

The Life Saving Service maintained beach patrols and practiced drills until 1915. At that time the United States Coast Guard came into being, coordinating the Life Saving Service, the Revenue Cutter Service, and the Lighthouse Service.

Today the United States Coast Guard conducts search and rescue missions with the latest equipment from Otis Air Force Base and from sea headquarters at Woods Hole, Chatham and Provincetown.

Crew members at one of the Cape Cod Life Saving Service stations on Cape Cod. The keeper (left) stayed year round. The surf men worked for ten months, patrolling the beach from dawn till dusk. Photograph courtesy of Tales of Cape Cod, Inc.

Surf boat on a beach cart ready for launching at the first news of a disaster. Photograph courtesy of Tales of Cape Cod, Inc.

Lifesaving crew ready with the breeches buoy. A Lyle gun was used to fire a line to a wrecked vessel. Seamen were then drawn to safety over the anchored line. Photograph courtesy of Tales of Cape Cod, Inc.

Lifesaving crew in action both patrolling and hauling in the lifesaving car. Photograph from Truro, Cape Cod by Shebnah Rich; courtesy of the Cape Cod Community College Library

A lifesaving crew practicing for a mission.
The rule book said, "You have to go out."
There was no reference to coming back.
Photograph courtesy of Tales of Cape
Cod, Inc.

The Pacific Guano Company on Penzance Point was instrumental in bringing the railroad from Monument Beach to Woods Hole in 1872. The company brought guano (bird roosts) from islands in the Pacific and Caribbean, mixed it with other ingredients from Sicily and Germany, added menhaden oil, and processed it all into fertilizer. Established in 1859, this extensive plant was built in 1863.

Summer residents were delighted when the guano works went out of business in 1889 and the stench from the factory was gone. Year-round residents were dismayed for many jobs were lost. Photograph courtesy of the Falmouth Historical Society

Change was very scarce in Centerville in the late 1800s, so F. G. Kelley made his own money for use in his country store. Photograph by Dick Holbrook; courtesy of John Howland Crocker

Good 5 for FIVE CENTS. PAYABLE IN CURRENT BANK BILLS AT MY COUNTER. F. G. Kelley. No. 107

GOOD 25 FOR Twentyfive cents. PAYABLE IN CURRENT Bank Bills. AT MY COUNTER. No. 107 F. G. Kelley.

GOOD 10 FOR TEN CENTS. PAYABLE IN CURRENT BANK BILLS AT MY COUNTER. No. 107 F. G. Kelley.

Gypsies were a common sight on the Cape in earlier days. The gypsy camp shown here was on the outskirts of Hyannis. Photograph donated by Carrie G. Harris; courtesy of the Cape Cod Community College Library

Alfred Crocker with his trotter (race horse) and sulky. Racing was a popular sport judging by the number of Trotting Park roads that now dot the Cape. Photograph of John Howland Crocker

The trotting park in East Falmouth at race time. Note the first primitive vans at right. Photograph courtesy of the Falmouth Historical Society

Racing was a very popular part of the annual Barnstable County Agricultural Society fair. There were plenty of onlookers in the late 1880s to cheer on their favorites. Photograph courtesy of the Trayser Museum

A baseball game in progress at the annual Barnstable County Agricultural Society Fair, Barnstable Village grounds. The society was founded in 1844 and grew in popularity until 1920. After a few declining years it was terminated in 1932, then reactivated until it became the popular event it is today. Photograph courtesy of the Trayser Museum

First
Swift
Plant
1867

One of the national businesses that had Cape Cod beginnings was Swift and Company, the Chicago meat packaging house. Gustavus Franklin Swift, a native of Sagamore, was a butcher in Barnstable. The location of his first plant is pictured here. Photograph courtesy of the Trayser Museum

Joseph Jefferson, a foremost American actor, in his favorite role of Rip Van Winkle. Jefferson was a fourth generation actor and became an instant success with his first appearance as Rip in Dio Boucicault's version of the Rip Van Winkle story in 1865.

He established a summer home on Buttermilk Bay in 1889 and became a close friend of President Grover Cleveland who summered nearby at Gray Gables. Photograph donated by Donald Jacobs; courtesy of the Bourne Town Archives

The Crow's Nest, summer home of actor Joseph Jefferson, with the actor pictured studying a script just before his death in 1905.

Jefferson established a large compound around his home, giving each of his five sons, his daughter, and his sister sites on which to build summer cottages. He insisted they spend summers at the Crow's Nest and delighted in having family and friends gather for games and charades. Photograph courtesy of the Bourne Town Archives

A view of the interior of the front hall at the Crows' Nest, home of actor Joseph Jefferson. In April 1893 the home burned, and many beautiful possessions were lost. The house was rebuilt, however, and the family gatherings continued each summer. Photograph courtesy of the Bourne Town Archives

A Bearse family reunion in the late 1800s. Photograph courtesy of the Trayser Museum

The members of the county agricultural society enjoy a picnic at Sandy Neck. Photograph donated by M. Holway; courtesy of the Trayser Museum

For seventy years this one-room district schoolhouse, built in 1869, fulfilled its function of educating the young. Successive Eastham generation learned "reading and writing and 'rithmetic." The picture of the class seated at desks was taken about 1890. The photo of the students with their wonderful hats is undated. Photographs courtesy of Sadie F. Flint

The Eastham schoolhouse now stands at the entrance of the Cape Cod National Seashore Park and is the home of the Eastham Historical Society. It contains an extensive collection of artifacts.

The entrance is framed by the jawbone of a whale, a typical feature of front yards long ago. A whale jawbone would be buried for a year to let insects pick it clean, then the whitened bone would make an arresting gate. Photograph by Al Flint

The store in the Craigville village center
was an offshoot of Hallett's country store
in Centerville. Sam and Moses Hallett
traveled between the two locations in summer making sure their famous peach ice
cream was always on hand. Photograph
courtesy of the Craigville Conference
Center

Chapter 8

Summer
Visitors,
Day Trippers

1872–1913

Some perceptive residents had glimmers of the rich veins to be mined from the natural beauties of the land. In 1872 the ambitious Hyannis Land Company acquired 1,000 acres on Barnstable's south shore. Hyannis Port was laid out much as it is today, with a hotel and a number of cottages.

That same year (1872) an ambitious development was put on the drawing board for Falmouth Heights. An adjoining pond was optimistically named "Elysian." Clergy and laymen of the Christian denomination acquired Strawberry Hill and laid out Craigville Village in back of crescent-shaped Craigville Beach. In 1873 the Christian Camp Meeting Association had two hotels, thirty-one cottages, and a tabernacle ready for summer camp meetings.

Enterprising Boston and Osterville men acquired acreage in Wianno and built Cotocheset House and a few summer homes that same year. Boston families, including Lowells, Coolidges, and Codmans, established a summer colony in Cotuit about this time. Similar pockets of summer folk found havens up and down Cape shores.

This was the era when families came for the summer to escape the hot cities. Pets, baggage, and people rode down on the railroad which by now had crept to Provincetown and had become indispensable. Met by horse-drawn "barges," the vacationers were trundled over the sandy roads to their beach homes. Fathers joined their families on weekends, coming via the "dude train."

Day trippers came as well as overnighters, and soon Cape Codders filled up their spare bedrooms with transients, set out jelly and vegetable stands, and peddled fresh-caught fish.

In the early 1900s, automobiles began to swarm onto the Cape like bees, buzzing down the sandy highways and seeking that elusive nectar, gasoline. The trains had reigned supreme until now and did for some decades yet. However, the motor car, which was destined to take over, was swarming noisily about in prophetic fashion.

But more than tourists were coming to the Cape. Hyannis had been chosen as the site of one of the state's four normal schools. Would-be teachers arrived in 1894 for the opening sessions held in three impressive brick buildings. Higher education had begun.

Woods Hole had become the setting for another unusual educational venture in 1873 when Harvard's Louis Agassiz collected a few students and taught marine biology on Penikese Island. Though the initial experiment failed after a few years, the Marine Biological Laboratory was to survive and become world famous.

Still another school of higher learning, which was to eventually locate on Cape Cod, was begun in 1891. An act of the legislature called into being the Massachusetts Nautical Training School to train the young to become officers in the United States Merchant Marine. Buzzards Bay was the final location of this school in 1948, though the six prior years were spent in Hyannis.

Almost simultaneously, modern communications came to the Cape and to the nation. In 1879 international news began flowing through an undersea cable from Brest, France, to the French Cable Station in Orleans, and was redirected to the country's nerve centers—New York City and Washington, D.C. From 1880 to 1940 this cable station was the main route for international communication.

But on a nearby bluff Guglielmo Marconi was already perfecting the wireless which would eventually supersede the cable. By 1901 Marconi had his first permanent radio station in South Wellfleet. Several years later, when communication was established with Cornwall, England, President Theodore Roosevelt and King Edward the VII of England exchanged greetings over 3,000 miles of air waves.

It was in this era that Grover Cleveland established the first summer White House on the Cape. Cleveland, who served as president of the United States from 1885 to 1889 and again from 1893 to 1897, purchased a home at the mouth of the Manomet River in 1890. Called Gray Gables, it was a welcome retreat from official duties during Cleveland's second term in office.

Other presidents visited the Cape. Ulysses S. Grant traveled its length in 1874. Theodore Roosevelt laid the cornerstone of the Pilgrim Monument in 1907 amid a spectacular naval display. William Howard Taft dedicated the monument in 1910. But half a century would elapse before another summer White House would be established here.

Authors have always visited this narrow land and waxed lyrical about its charms, beginning with William Wood, who toured the new plantations in the early 1630s. On his return to England he published in *New England's Prospect* a complete description of the flora, fauna, and people, calling it "for certain the best ground and sweetest climate in all these parts bearing the name of New England."

A later famed visitor was Henry David Thoreau who was tremendously impressed with the great beach at Nauset: "The breakers looked like droves of a thousand wild horses of Neptune, rushing to shore with their white manes streaming far behind."

But not all authors were tourists or day trippers. It was two native-born authors who brought the Cape into prominence during this era. Joseph Crosby Lincoln published *Cape Cod Ballads* in 1902, but it was the novel *Cap'n Eri* which made the characters of his Brewster boyhood famed throughout the nation. Thornton Waldo Burgess, born several years after Lincoln, created characters from his early observations of animals in the Briar Patch of Sandwich. His "Bedtime Stories" were syndicated in newspapers, leading in 1918 to the first of his many books.

The 200th anniversary of the founding of the town of Falmouth (1686 to 1886) was celebrated in grand fashion. In this mammoth tent can be seen at each place a box lunch and an anniversary mug. Photograph courtesy of the Falmouth Historical Society

Yarmouth was the next town to celebrate an anniversary when in September 1889 it observed the 250th year of its founding, or the Quarter-Millenial Celebration.

Flags were hung across Hallett Street, which according to Ruth Bray, writing in the tercentenary booklet was "the upper end of Yarmouth Street" or the present Route 6A. It was so called because it was practically an all Hallett neighborhood. Photograph from The Celebration of the Two Hundred and Fiftieth Anniversary of the Founding of Yarmouth; courtesy of Jack Smith

This old time version of the school bus is the barge which transported high school students to Hyannis from Osterville, via Centerville in 1910. It is pictured in front of the old tin shop in Centerville. Photograph courtesy of the Centerville Historical Society

When the tin peddler's cart came jingling down the road, residents emerged to barter and buy the bright new tinware and other necessary household items. Photograph from September 1915 Cape Cod *magazine*

The graduating class of Barnstable High School in 1908 with Principal L. M. Boody in the center front. Photograph courtesy of the Trayser Museum

The beach and cottages at Hyannisport around the turn of the century. Note the many windmills on the skyline. The point of land to the left is the location of today's Kennedy Compound. Photograph courtesy of the Trayser Museum

Beach & Cottages, Hyannisport, Mass.

The Observatory was part of the real estate development at Falmouth Heights in 1872. It was used as a chapel and has been torn down in recent years. Photograph courtesy of the Falmouth Historical Society

The ambitious land development centered around Observatory Hill was planned in 1872. This was the basis for a grand summer colony which persisted for many years in Falmouth Heights. It was typical of developments in other parts of the Cape about the same time. Photograph of map by Dick Holbrook; courtesy of the Falmouth Historical Society

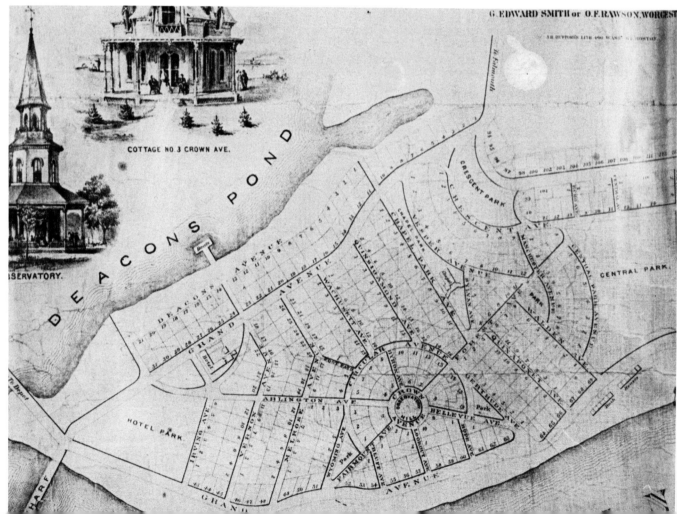

COTTAGE NO. 3 CROWN AVE.

OBSERVATORY.

DEACONS POND

This photo shows the French Cable Station in Orleans, built in 1890 by the French Telegraph Cable Company, with some of the construction workers. The station is now a museum and is open during the summer. The original equipment is still on view in this historic communication spot which is on the National Register of Historic Places. Photograph courtesy of the French Cable Station Museum

This telephone book of 1886 included Cape Cod even though the phone company was based in New Bedford. Photograph by Dick Holbrook; courtesy of the Cape Cod Community College Library

THE EXCELSIOR TELEPHONE,

This recently perfected Telephone is entirely different in its construction from any other instrument ever placed before the public, for conveying the human voice to a distance.— For lines of one or two miles, and shorter distances, this is by far the most effective instrument known to science. No electricity or magnet is used; it acts on the well known principal of vibration alone.

By its means, conversation can be carried on, over a wire of a mile or more in length, with the same facility as though the parties were face to face in the same room. No expensive call bells are required and consequently no batteries.— A simple "halloo" is sufficient to call the attention of the distant party.

These important and wonderful results have been attained by the peculiar construction of the instrument which is modeled after the human ear.

This instrument has been patented and does not infringe on the Bell or Edison Telephone in any manner, and unlike either of them it is *sold* at a very low price.

In several counties in Ohio, where the instrument was invented, many Merchants, Lawyers, Doctors, etc., have connected their residences, and places of business, and the neighboring farmers have communications between each other, by means of this cheap and effective little instrument.

Station Agents on Railroads find it a great convenience, enabling them to communicate between Passenger and Freight departments, and in some instances their residences also.

I will forward by express, to any address for $5, and 25 cts., return charges C. O. D., one pair Excelsior Telephones with full directions for putting up. It takes one pound of No. 19 copper wire to go 13 rods. I can furnish it at present at   cts. per lb.; Insulators or holders   cts. each, one is required at each post or rest, which should be 12 rods apart.

Direct orders to,

ARTHUR E. HOYT, Agent,
Atkinson Depot, N. H.

The telephone was marketed on Cape Cod by a New Hampshire agent in 1885. The flyer was printed by the Patriot Press. Photograph by Dick Holbrook; courtesy of John Howland Crocker

The extensive Cape Cod directory of 1886 as pictured in the Southern Massachusetts Telephone Company book. Photographs by Dick Holbrook; courtesy of the Cape Cod Community Library

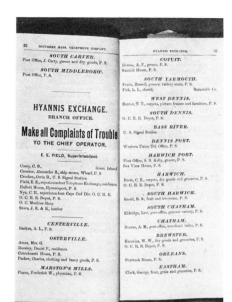

The first telephone switchboard in Hyannis, 1892. Photograph by Dick Holbrook; courtesy of the Trayser Museum

A ring on this vintage telephone got you "central." Photograph by Dick Holbrook; courtesy of the Trayser Museum

Harriet Crocker is shown on her bicycle in Barnstable in July 1896. Photograph courtesy of John Howland Crocker

Hyannis Normal School students celebrated May Day at the turn of the century. Photograph courtesy of Tales of Cape Cod, Inc.

This long ago game of croquet took place in Brewster. Photograph from the Donald Doane Memorial Collection; courtesy of Tales of Cape Cod, Inc.

Old Home Week was a popular time each year for families to gather in reunion. At this Old Home Week picnic the children's table is under watchful eyes. Photograph from August 1914 Cape Cod magazine

The English man-of-war Somerset was wrecked off Truro during the American Revolution. It was buried by the action of shifting sands and tides. In 1886 high tides and furious seas tore away the sandy shroud, and relic hunters descended. W. G. Gold donated this 1886 picture of a party of souvenir hunters. The skeleton of the old ship has since reappeared in 1925 and in 1973. Photograph by Nickerson; courtesy of the Cape Cod Community College Library

1. Alfred Howland
2. Harry Ryder
3. Carlton Ryder
4. Elmer Hallet
5. Bill Cahoon
6. N.T. Hallet
7. John Brice
8. Herbert Vincent
9. Charles Swift

The beach was a popular place in summer, though bathers were not as scantily clad as today. The Christian Camp Meeting Association purchased the central part of Craigville Beach in 1888 for $846.95! Photograph courtesy of the Craigville Conference Center

Bands have always been popular since instruments arrived on the Cape. Most towns have a band shell where outdoor concerts take place in summer. The Yarmouth Brass Band is pictured here about 1880. Photograph courtesy of the Historical Society of Old Yarmouth

In 1897 a club house was built on Brewster Beach. It was connected with the Brewster Golf Course and was the scene of many social events. Photograph from the Donald Doane Memorial Collection; courtesy of Tales of Cape Cod, Inc.

A tennis tournament took place in August 1900 at the Falmouth home of the Honorable Richard Olney who was secretary of state in the administration of President Grover Cleveland. Olney was a real sports enthusiast, playing tennis several mornings a week every summer. According to the local newspaper, those tennis matches were "a social institution in the town." Mrs. Olney is shown here on the far right. Photograph courtesy of the Falmouth Historical Society

Movie theaters came to the Cape in the early 1900s. The Empire Theater began in Falmouth in 1910, showing pictures two nights a week. The first movie operator was Bert Warren (left), who moonlighted from his regular job with the old Cape and Vineyard Electric Company. The owner of the theater was Bill Snow (right). Photograph courtesy of the Falmouth Historical Society

Captain Edward Penniman made a fortune as a whaling ship master. In 1876 he retired and built this French empire (Victorian) style house which is unlike most Cape Cod homes. People came for miles to watch its construction in Eastham. Now owned by the Cape Cod National Seashore Park, it is kept in excellent condition as is the matching barn and the whalebone gateway in the rear. Photograph from A Trip Around Cape Cod by E. G. Perry; courtesy of the Trayser Museum

Most of Eastham's residents attended the annual picnic of the Universalist Sunday school. At this gathering, taken around 1910, the happy picnickers are standing in front of the Coast Guard Station. Captain Edward Penniman, retired whaler and probably the town's wealthiest citizen, is pictured with his wife Augusta standing in the right front. Francis W. Smith and his wife Sarah flank the picnickers, standing on the extreme left and right. Smith was a large landowner and raised turnips and asparagus for the markets. Photograph courtesy of Sadie F. Flint, the little blonde girl standing center front

The H. V. Lawrence florist shop on Depot Street in Falmouth was founded in 1886 by Harry Vincent Lawrence and is pictured here in its early days. The business is now owned by Cameron and Margaret Gifford, who purchased it in March 1977. Photograph courtesy of the Falmouth Historical Society

A Falmouth lumberyard in the early 1900s. Photograph courtesy of the Falmouth Historical Society

Fishermen drawing the weir net close off Eastham about 1910. Photograph courtesy of Sadie F. Flint

Francis W. Smith harvesting fish from his Eastham weir in 1910. Photograph courtesy of Sadie F. Flint

Weir fishing took place in off-shore Cape Cod waters for many years. The weir arrangement is shown here at low tide off Brewster in the early 1900s. Photograph from the Donald Doane Memorial Collection; courtesy of Tales of Cape Cod, Inc.

When the fish were contained in the weirs, horses and wagons were used to load them for market, as in this Brewster scene. Photograph from the Donald Doane Memorial Collection; courtesy of Tales of Cape Cod, Inc.

Dr. George W. Doane of Hyannis showed the chaise in which he made his daily calls in winter. He practiced in the late 1800s and died in 1905. Photograph courtesy of O. Herbert McKenney

This grain and coal company, owned by H. B. Chase, who had many sidelines, was pictured in a directory of businesses in the Hyannis, Hyannisport, Osterville, and Wianno areas about 1919. It was sold for twenty-five cents by the publisher, George Richardson of New York. Photograph courtesy of the Trayser Museum

Residents came to view the damage after the fire of December 1904, which devastated the east end of Hyannis. Fifteen stores were burned, and damages were estimated at $150,000. Photograph courtesy of Edward B. Gillis

Rebirth was quick after the Hyannis fire of 1904. William P. Bearse is pictured erecting a building in the fire-ravaged district. Photograph courtesy of O. Herbert McKenney

Many Irish people came to Hyannis to work on the railroad in the late 1850s. Second generation Irish became grocers or bakers. Some companies were mobile like Murphy's Health Ice Cream, seen here with its wagons on Main Street, Hyannis, before the fire of 1904. Photograph courtesy of Edward R. Gillis

Much modernized, the store is shown in 1962. Harry Bearse (center) had purchased the store in 1932. Earl Baker stands at the left, while present owner Thurlow "Buss" Bearse is at right. Bradford's Hardware now consists of three units: the Hyannis store (above), the Harwichport store, and Abco Rental Center. Photograph by the Kelsey Studio; Melvin Howard, photographer; courtesy of Thurlow Bearse

Bradford's Hardware Store is one of the businesses begun in the last century which has grown with the years and the times. Begun in Hyannis in 1865 by Alexander Cash, it became Myron Bradford's in 1892. The staff, pictured here in 1918, includes (left to right) Myron Bradford, Ernest Bradford, Harry Bearse, and Ike Baker. Photograph courtesy of O. Herbert McKenney

One of the first planes to fly on the Cape was this flimsy looking airplane flown on Scraggy Neck, Bourne, in 1912. The object of much curiosity, the plane had pontoons for water landings and "a seat hanging in mid-air attached to not much of anything." It was a two motor job. Each motor was started by twisting a propeller. The pontoons were removable, and wheels underneath allowed it to take off from a field as well as from water. Photograph courtesy of the Bourne Town Archives

Charles Carroll Jones is pictured about 1890 with his work horses on the Main Street of Barnstable Village. Photograph courtesy of Patricia Anderson

Charles Carroll Jones of Barnstable is shown with his dog on his boat the Sea Gull, Barnstable Harbor, 1920s. Jones went to sea in his early years, then became a farmer, contractor, and teamster. According to his obituary in the Barnstable Patriot, January 2, 1930, he sailed around the world a half a dozen times before marrying Hester M. Joy and raising a family. Photograph courtesy of Patricia Anderson

The county officials pictured about 1900: standing (left to right) are Thomas Soule, commissioner; Clarendon Freeman, registrar of probate; Freeman L. Lothrop, judge of probate; John A. Holway, registrar of deeds, Henry Percival, high sheriff; Lafayette Chase, commissioner. Seated (left to right): unidentified assistant jailer; Captain Allen Nickerson, jailer; Charles Thompson, commissioner; and Alfred Crocker, clerk of the superior court. Photograph courtesy of John Howland Crocker

Katharine Lee Bates was born in this home just off the Falmouth Green while her father was pastor of the Congregational church. It is now a museum owned by the Falmouth Historical Society

Joseph Crosby Lincoln was born in this house on Route 6A in Brewster in 1870. Though he left the Cape at age thirteen, he often returned to visit his many relatives. In later years he summered in Chatham. Photograph courtesy of Tales of Cape Cod, Inc.

Lincoln eventually wrote fifty books, including three with his son Freeman Lincoln. The famous author is pictured here about 1910. Photograph courtesy of Tales of Cape Cod, Inc.

142

Thornton Waldo Burgess, born in 1874, spent his early years in Sandwich, leaving after his high school graduation for a career in journalism. Though his fame largely rests on his animal tales for children, he was gifted in other lines. He wrote advertising copy, produced poetry, and wrote a book for the Boy Scouts as well as a bird book for children. His eventual book total was 151. He also gathered a wide audience on radio station WBZ in Springfield and spent his last years in Hamden. Photograph courtesy of the Thornton W. Burgess Society, Inc.

Katharine Lee Bates, born in 1859 in Falmouth, was a famous poet, author, and teacher. She was a professor at Wellesley College. Though she authored some thirteen books, her fame largely rests on her poem "America the Beautiful." Photograph courtesy of the Falmouth Historical Society

The Alice May Davenport out of Bath, Maine, was stranded in Cape Cod Bay January 1905. The schooner anchored, but the chains parted and she was driven to rest 300 yards off North Dennis shore. Because of the fierce winter weather, the schooner was not freed until March. Photograph courtesy of Tales of Cape Cod, Inc.

The Wing Family of America held its first reunion in 1902 at the old family homestead then owned and occupied by Alvin T. Wing. Photograph courtesy of the Wing Family of America

The Old Colony Club pictured in 1904. Photograph by Small; courtesy of the Bourne Historical Society

Main Street, Hyannis, after a snowfall in the 1880s. Photograph courtesy of the Trayser Museum

The steamer Ruth on Wakeby Lake, South Sandwich. Captain Benjamin F. Boardley was her skipper. This picture was taken prior to 1898. From A Trip Around Cape Cod by E. G. Perry; courtesy of the Trayser Museum

The map of the Cape Cod and Old Colony Railroad was made after the railroad reached Provincetown and Falmouth, but before it reached Chatham in 1887. Photograph from Truro, Cape Cod by Shebnah Rich; courtesy of the Cape Cod Community College Library

*F*lag man at the Hyannis road crossing in Barnstable in July 1896. Photograph courtesy of John Howland Crocker

*T*he Flying Dude *was a special train chartered by the wealthy folk to shuttle between Boston and their summer homes along Buzzards Bay shore. One small boy recalls in amazement watching it "streak by in a cloud of dust at a mile a minute clip." The Dude ran from 1884 to 1914 and, in spite of its speed, never had a mishap. Photograph courtesy of the Falmouth Historical Society*

*A*ugustus Messer, dignified conductor of *the* Flying Dude, *was the first conductor to bring a train into Woods Hole. He was known for his polished attire, a blue frock coat with sparkling brass buttons, and usually a fresh flower in his buttonhole. He worked thirty-two years on the Boston-Woods Hole run, with fourteen of these on the Dude. Photograph courtesy of the Bourne Town Archives*

146

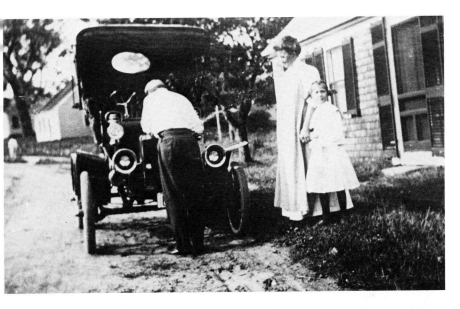

A two cylinder Maxwell was giving a bit of trouble in 1901 to Alfred Crocker as his wife Katherine and daughter Ruth looked on. Photograph courtesy of John Howland Crocker

Ruth Crocker at the wheel of her father's two cylinder Maxwell in 1901. Photograph courtesy of John Howland Crocker

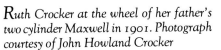

This 1908 photo of S. C. Burgess in his Stevens Dureyea automobile was taken in Falmouth. Photograph courtesy of the Falmouth Historical Society

During the summer in the 1920s, swimming, barbecues, bacon bats, and picnics caused traffic jams at the beach. The bathhouses of the Christian Camp Meeting Association can be seen in the background. These are still available today, though in more modern form. Photograph courtesy of the Craigville Conference Center

The Cape Cod Laundry, pictured here in the early 1900s, was a West Yarmouth establishment. It became part of the Acme Laundry business during World War II. Leo Vernon Eldridge had founded Acme Laundry in Chatham in 1916. When World War II came, the government "seized by lease" both the Chatham laundry and one in Falmouth also owned by Eldridge.

These two laundries were operated around the clock to take care of laundry needs of prisoners and soldiers at Camp Edwards. With much business and no facilities, Eldridge bought the Cape Cod Laundry and expanded it. Acme Laundry now has about ten outlets and is operated by Kenneth Eldridge, his brother Leo Eldridge, and son Kevin. Photograph courtesy of the Trayser Museum

Trolley cars ran from New Bedford to Monument Beach from 1902 to 1914. They regularly crossed the trestle at the Narrows Bridge at Buttermilk Bay, clattered along Electric Avenue and Main Street of Buzzards Bay and over Old Bridge Road. They then crossed a small bridge and trestle near where the present Bourne Post Office stands. The trolleys then traveled across Bourne Corners and up County Road to Monument Beach. Here the yellow cars would reverse for the return trip.

There were closed cars in winter and open cars with safety rails in summer. The creation of the Cape Cod Canal ended this mode of travel on Cape Cod. Although a trolley line ran briefly from Plymouth to Sagamore in 1917, it never really found a following. Photograph courtesy of the Bourne Town Archives

*S*tephen Grover Cleveland was president of the United States from 1885 to 1889 and again from 1893 to 1897. He was a summer resident of Bourne. Photograph courtesy of the Bourne Town Archives

*W*hen President Grover Cleveland came to his summer home by train, he alighted at this tiny railroad station. In recent years the Bourne Historical Society raised funds to move the station to the grounds of the Aptucxet Trading Post, where it can be viewed in summer. Photograph courtesy of the Bourne Town Archives

*T*he Oneida, the presidential yacht of Grover Cleveland, was owned by Commodore Ely Benedict of the New York Yacht Club, who put it at the president's disposal. It was so often in Buzzards Bay that most people thought it belonged to Cleveland.

It was on this yacht, during a Fourth of July weekend, that the president was operated on for a malignant cancer of the mouth. The entire incident was kept quiet until after the president was back in the White House and ready to address Congress in late August. Photograph courtesy of the Bourne Town Archives

149

Gray Gables, the home of Grover Cleveland, who was twenty-second and twenty-fourth president of the United States, was the first Summer White House on Cape Cod. Cleveland's daughter Marion was born here, and the president enjoyed many hours of his favorite sport—fishing. For many years afterwards, until it burned, Gray Gables was a summer inn. Courtesy of the Bourne Town Archives

A glimpse into President Grover Cleveland's personal economic outlook is given in this handwritten letter to William Crump, builder of Gray Gables. The president wrote that the estimate was too high and that he was giving up part of his plans for building. William Crump, Jr. gave the letter to the Bourne Town Archives. Photograph courtesy of the Bourne Town Archives

President Theodore Roosevelt is shown flanked by Senator Henry Cabot Lodge (left), Governor Curtis Guild, Jr. of Massachusetts (right) and J. Henry Sears (far right), president of the Cape Cod Pilgrim Memorial Association. President Roosevelt participated in the laying of the cornerstone of the Pilgrim Monument on August 20, 1907. Following a series of addresses, the grand master of the Masons in Massachusetts, Most Worshipful J. Albert Baker, and 100 Masons led the ceremony of placing a copper box containing many items in the hole and laying the stone. Photograph from The Pilgrims and Their Monument by Edmund J. Carpenter

Executive Mansion
Washington
October 25, 1895

Wm. R. Crump, Esq.
Dear Sir:

The plans and specifications for the house and addition to the barn which you sent me are altogether too elaborate and expensive.

I have abandoned building the addition to the barn for the present and if I build a house it must be a cheaper one than you have proposed.

A dwelling plenty big enough and good enough ought to be built for less than $1200. I intend it for Mr. Wright and in talking with him about it he has always put the probable cost considerably below the amount above stated.

Yours truly,
S/Grover Cleveland

The U.S.S. Mayflower *brought President Theodore Roosevelt to the ceremonies accompanied by "eight great battleships and a fleet of gaudily bedecked pleasure yachts." The* Mayflower *steamed through the line of battleships followed by a flotilla of destroyers. "The great guns boomed a welcome" to Provincetown Harbor as the* Mayflower *anchored in as near as possible to the position of her namesake ship. "It seemed as if the* Mayflower *would be lost to view in the great haze of powder smoke," wrote Carpenter. Photograph from* The Pilgrims and Their Monument *by Edmund J. Carpenter*

President of the United States William Howard Taft dedicated the monument on August 15, 1910, the anniversary of the day the Pilgrims sailed from Southampton, England, for America. Charles W. Eliot, president emeritus of Harvard University, gave the major address.

Here President J. Henry Sears of the Cape Cod Pilgrim Memorial Association and Governor Eben S. Draper of Massachusetts are ready to greet President and Mrs. Taft as they come up the gangplank from the Mayflower. *As before, the Atlantic fleet of eight battleships was in the Provincetown Harbor and gave the customary military honors.*

Evening festivities included a grand ball in the Town Hall and a magnificent illumination in the harbor. Every house blazed with light, and "the great monument itself was decorated throughout its entire height with electric lights, more than one thousand lamps being employed," according to Carpenter. Photograph from The Pilgrims and Their Monument *by Edmund J. Carpenter*

Pilgrim Monument as seen from the ancient hilltop cemetery. Photograph by Dick Holbrook

The Cape Cod Canal under construction. Digging began in 1809 when August Belmont financed the tremendous project. Photograph courtesy of the Bourne Town Archives

Chapter 9

Changes: A Canal and a War

1914 - 1918

One of the two startling changes that occurred within these years was the cutting of the Cape Cod Canal, which made this peninsula an island. Men had long dreamed of digging a channel between the Scusset Creek and the Manomet River. When the Pilgrims traded with the Dutch of New Amsterdam at Aptucxet Trading Post, they portaged small boats across the marsh and lowland and talked of connecting the waterways. Later George Washington saw its advantages and in June 1776 recommended a survey by engineers.

Every few years thereafter another gentleman or a different company determined to do the deed. In 1898 the *Barnstable Patriot* noted seven canal proposals before the state legislature, commenting, "Meanwhile, despite all threats, the Cape hangs on to the mainland with the grim determination characteristic of its people."

Financier August Belmont finally succeeded in creating the canal, beginning in June 1909 and finishing on April 21, 1914. Preparations for commercial use followed, and Belmont and his party celebrated that Fourth of July by rowing the first boat through the channel. The passageway at last allowed ships to pass safely up the coast without rounding the treacherous shoals off the outer Cape—the graveyard of so many vessels. For fourteen years the canal was privately operated, then it was purchased by the United States government.

The other major change was caused by World War I. Although the fighting was overseas, this land which protrudes 100 miles into the ocean was both valuable and vulnerable. It was strategically placed for the movement of troops and equipment overseas. It was thus a target for the enemy—especially near the canal.

Many men and women answered the nation's call to serve overseas, and some made the supreme sacrifice. Those who weren't on active duty patrolled the coast in their own craft. Others worked at the military installations, helped with Liberty Loan and War Savings Stamps drives, and contributed to the work of the Red Cross and Salvation Army.

Until this era, most of the Cape villages, especially those along the north shore, had retained their sleepy look, changing little outwardly. Here and there a few new homes and stores were constructed. Occasionally a new white steeple had pushed upward through the foliage. By this time Methodists, Unitarians, Catholics, and Episcopalians were contributing to the ecumenical patchwork quilt. At the turn of the century a profusion of smaller denominations added more color.

Hyannis had changed most radically. In the 1800s there had been only a few dwellings clustered near Lewis Bay. With the construction of the breakwater at Hyannis Port and the building of the railroad spur directly to the water, the harbor became the principal stopping point for coasters, packets, freight vessels, steamers, and passenger ships. During one northeaster 100 vessels rode out the storm. From 1900 on, Hyannis, one of the town of Barnstable's seven villages, became the business hub of the Cape.

World War I accelerated change not only in Hyannis but in Falmouth, Bourne, and Sandwich, which were near the Cape Cod Canal.

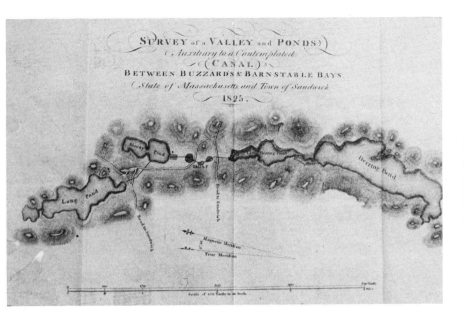

Survey of a valley and ponds done in 1825 in preparation for a canal between Buzzards and Barnstable bays which had actually been contemplated since the Pilgrim days. Photograph by Dick Holbrook; courtesy of Cape Cod Community Library

Profile of the proposed route for a canal between Buzzards and Barnstable bays. This interesting view of the elevations was done in 1825. This and the other two maps were drawn by Major P. H. Perrault of the United States Army Corps of Engineers following his 1824 survey. Photograph by Dick Holbrook; courtesy of the Cape Cod Community College Library

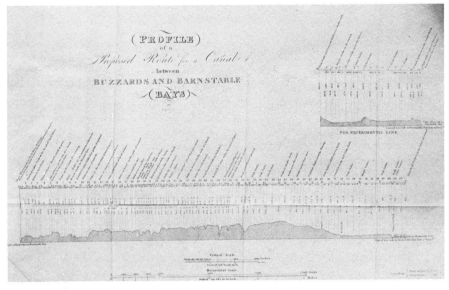

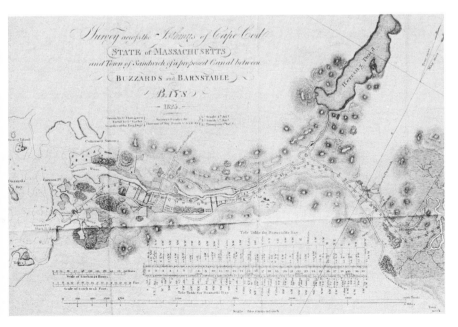

The general survey of the isthmus (also 1825) was the third map made in preparation for a possible canal. These very rare maps on fragile paper are part of the fine collection in the Cape Cod room of the Cape Cod Community College. Photograph by Dick Holbrook; courtesy of the Cape Cod Community College Library

This photo of Monument River near Collins Farm Crossing shows the peaceful stream before the creation of the Cape Cod Canal. Photograph by Channing Howard; courtesy of the Bourne Town Archives

Cutting the last dike in the Cape Cod Canal, April 1914. Photograph by Channing Howard; courtesy of the Bourne Town Archives

Cutting the Last Dike in Cape Cod Canal, Apr., 1914

Dignitaries gathered to celebrate the opening of the Cape Cod Canal, July 29, 1914. Photograph courtesy of the Bourne Town Archives

The first bridge at Sagamore lifts to let two tugs through. Photograph courtesy of the Bourne Town Archives

Cruise ship in the Cape Cod Canal. Photograph courtesy of the Cape Cod Chamber of Commerce

The verticle lift bridge over the canal was completed in 1935 at a cost of $1,800,000. The 544-foot span, when raised, is 135 feet above high water. In this picture the span has been lowered by cables suspended from the towers to permit a train to pass. Photograph courtesy of the U. S. Corps of Engineers, Department of the Army

The control room of the bridge has complicated equipment to aid operator Larry Genander of Conrail in watching for both ships and trains. Photograph courtesy of the U. S. Corps of Engineers, Department of the Army

A Brazilian tanker is helped through the Canal by the Corps of Engineers' tug, Bourne. Oil tankers, barges, and ships carrying liquid propane stream steadily through the widest artificial waterway in the world today along with a multitude of pleasure craft. Photograph courtesy of the U. S. Corps of Engineers, Department of the Army

Chronology of Cape Cod Canal

1626   Canal suggested by Pilgrim Governor William Bradford.

1697   Massachusetts General Court appointed a committee to study feasibility of cutting a passage.

1776   Massachusetts General Court passed a resolution suggesting a canal across the isthmus.

1791   Another resolution by the court authorized a survey by James Winthrop.

1801   The town of Sandwich approved the petition of Thomas Parker to build a thirty-two-foot-wide waterway with adjacent tow path.

1860   Massachusetts Governor Nathaniel Banks in his inaugural address called for another look at the canal project.

1870   Cape Cod Ship Canal Company granted charter to dig the canal and after a ten year delay began September 15, 1880. Over 100 Italian laborers were hired to dig with picks, shovels, and wheelbarrows. Work was abandoned in November when money ran out.

1904   August Perry Belmont became interested and scheduled a survey.

1907   Belmont's Cape Cod Construction Company began to dig on July 29.

1914   Official opening of the canal on July 29.

1918   Canal co-opted by the U. S. government during World War I.

1928   U. S. Army Corps of Engineers takes over operation in April from August Belmont's Boston, Cape Cod and New York Canal Company.

1935   Modern Bourne and Sagamore Highway bridges completed in August. Vertical Lift Railroad Bridge completed in December.

1940   U. S. Army Corps of Engineers completes widening and deepening of canal. Canal now the widest sea-level waterway with controlling depth of thirty-two feet at mean low water.

1973   Installation in September of centralized ship traffic control system. Operation now by an integrated system of radar, closed circuit television surveillance, and multi-channel VHF-FM radio communication equipment.

1980   Passage in July of new stricter navigational regulations. Engineer in charge has more authority in management of vessels. In August the east end of canal deepened to forty feet at mean low water to allow for offloading of deep draft tankers at Canal Electric Company Terminal.

1981   Major rehabilitation of Bourne Bridge completed in May.

1982   Major rehabilitation of Sagamore Bridge scheduled for completion in December.

Information since April 1928 supplied by F. N. Ciccone, U.S. Army Corps of Engineers; previous data from Cape Cod Canal *by Robert Farson*

The imposing granite Barnstable County Courthouse, built in 1832, was the setting for the draft board during World War I. Registration of all men between the ages of twenty-one and thirty-one was taken here under a board headed by Captain C. Lawrence Barry of Craigville, a retired Marine Corps officer. The first quota raised was of 164 men from the Cape and the Islands. They gathered in Hyannis on September 22, 1917, at the Masonic hall and next morning departed for Camp Devens by special train. This was repeated several more times before the armistice whistles sounded. Photograph courtesy of the Cape Cod Community Library

Major General Clarence R. Edwards, commander of the famed Twenty-sixth (Yankee) Infantry Division of Massachusetts, under whom many Cape Codders served in World War I. Camp Edwards was later named for the general. Photograph courtesy of the Department of the Army, Camp Edwards Headquarters

Ruth Crocker was in charge of the Liberty Loan Drive. The public was admitted free to the War Exhibit train, but salespersons were on hand to sell bonds as the people viewed the exhibits of World War I memorabilia. Photograph courtesy of John Howland Crocker

163

A naval air station was established in 1919 at what is now Eastward Point in Chatham. This blimp hangar, pictured in the spring of 1931 or 32, housed dirigibles. There were smaller hangars for seaplanes as well as many subsidiary buildings. Since the station was designed for use during the First World War, activity ceased soon after 1920, and eventually the area was privately developed for homes. Photograph courtesy of John Howland Crocker

The Barnstable High School baseball team of 1916. The front row (left to right) includes Russell Starck, Hugh Ferguson, Nelson Bearse and Fred Nute; the back row includes (left to right) Robert Elliott, Stuart Bradford, Carl Starck, Roy Maher, and Carroll Stevens. Photograph courtesy of the Trayser Museum

Of the Bourne High School class of 1918 only two can be identified: Edward Avery (first on the right) and Elsa Perry (seated). Perhaps the members were solemn because they wondered what was ahead for them in that war year. Photograph donated by Vesta Braley; courtesy of the Bourne Town Archives

Photographer and farmer met and ex-changed views about the latest in photo-graphic equipment in the early 1900s. Photograph from the Bourne Historical Society Collection; courtesy of the Bourne Town Archives

Chapter 10

The Modern Era

1919-1940

When the armistice was signed in 1918 and a semblance of normalcy returned to the country, people flocked back to the golden sands and inviting waters of Cape Cod to forget the war. Soon the cash registers of the crowded resorts were jingling. A few forward-looking citizens realized the importance of working together to direct and bolster this fledgling tourist industry. In April 1921, seventy-five men and women gathered in Hyannis, and the Cape Cod Chamber of Commerce was born. The economy continued to escalate and was only temporarily halted by the Wall Street crash of 1929.

It was during the following Great Depression that Cape Codders fully appreciated their surroundings. While city people queued up in bread lines, Cape folk secured food from the land and the sea. They caught fish, dug clams, and lived out of their gardens both summer and winter. Techniques born from long years of homesteading brought security many city dwellers did not know.

The population still numbered around 27,000 but steadily climbed after 1920. Some who added to the census figures were ethnic groups from overseas. Sailors from Portugal and the Azores were earlier comers to Provincetown and Falmouth, drawn by the whaling and fishing industries. Finns had arrived in the mid-1800s, jumping ship to try their luck ashore at farming, brick making, and bog work. The Irish had come from Boston when help was needed at the Sandwich glass works.

In 1903 Greek immigrants had arrived, eventually centralizing around their first church, the St. George Greek Orthodox in Hyannis, built in 1931. A sizable Jewish population gathered, meeting for worship in their Hyannis synagogue, which was erected in 1933. The Finns had gravitated to West Barnstable Village, erecting churches and community halls. They perpetuated their language in worship into this mid-century.

Portuguese-speaking citizens developed their own settlements in East Falmouth, Provincetown, and Falmouth. Their heritage remained so strong that mass was celebrated in Portuguese at St. Anthony's Catholic Church in East Falmouth until recent years. Some blacks had arrived in pre-Civil War days, either as slaves or as escapees from Southern slavery. More arrived in the 1900s to assist in the local work force, settling down to take their places in the business and social life. The result was a pleasing patchwork of colors and nationalities living together. By 1940 the earlier population decline had reversed and the pre-Civil War level was exceeded with 37,295 citizens.

Paradoxically, the ocean, which had originally been the Cape's economic mainstay, came into its own again in new and different ways. After the Great Depression, sailors with dimming memories of coastal trade used their skills to captain yachts for the growing wealthy class. Others skippered party boats, taking enthusiasts deep-sea fishing. Still others ran ferry lines to nearby islands and directed charter boats. Yacht racing, which had begun in the 1880s, now had thousands of fans in all sizes of crafts, including Crosby Catboats and Wianno Seniors. All this and the related trades brought prosperity.

The increase in population created a need for health services. The Cape Cod Hospital began in 1920 in a frame house with fourteen beds. By 1932 it had metamorphosed into a brick establishment with sixty-five beds.

Social activities had increased also. A social/agricultural county-wide event, the Barnstable Agricultural Fair was held annually for several decades at the fairgrounds in Barnstable Village overlooking the old Common Fields. Threatened with extinction and dissolved in 1932, it was happily revived for the town of Barnstable's Tercentenary in 1939. Gaining new life, it continued and grew into today's annual event on fairgrounds in Hatchville, drawing contestants and visitors from afar.

The long history of theater, so integral to the Cape, had had its roots in Provincetown in 1916 when the Provincetown Players staged one of budding playwright Eugene O'Neill's plays on a rustic wharf. But summer theater really emerged nationwide when Raymond Moore opened the Cape Playhouse in Dennis with *The Guardsmen*, starring Basil Rathbone. The stellar programming of this first professional summer theater set the pattern for many other resort theaters.

Richard Aldrich opened the Falmouth Playhouse, one of the most beautiful summer theaters anywhere, in 1949. Then Aldrich and his wife, actress Gertrude Lawrence, brought tent theater to Hyannis in 1950 with the opening of the Cape Cod Music Circus (forerunner of today's Melody Tent).

Theater was not confined to the summer, however, for soon the Barnstable Comedy Club, begun in 1922, was offering workshops and at least three prime productions on the "off season." This oldest amateur theater group in the country was joined by the Chatham Drama Guild and the Falmouth Drama Guild.

These were the main stems from which many more theater groups would flower, some with year-round activity, as the population continued to grow.

Quohauging at Barlow's Town Landing in Pocasset is an example of a perennial Cape activity. Photograph donated by Clifford Wise; courtesy of the Bourne Town Archives

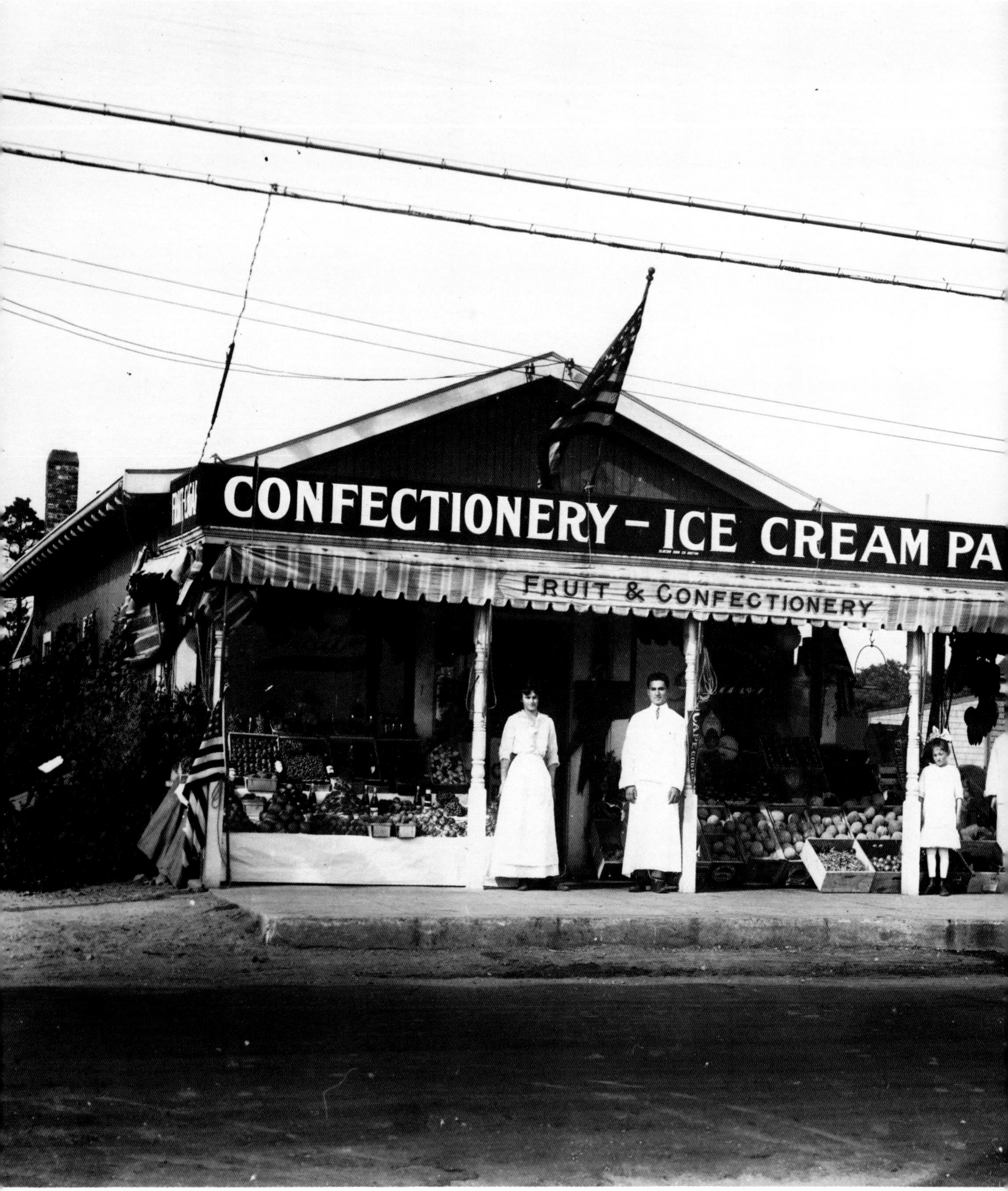
CONFECTIONERY – ICE CREAM PA
FRUIT & CONFECTIONERY

An early business on Main Street, Buzzards Bay—a fruit and confectionary shop photographed in the early 1900s. Photograph from the Bourne Historical Society Collection; courtesy of the Bourne Town Archives

Henry Fonda and his teen-age daughter Jane appeared together in The Male Animal at the Cape Playhouse in Dennis in 1956. This was Jane's first appearance with her father. Photograph by Percy Williams

Bournehurst-on-the-Canal was a dancing pavilion where famous-name bands played. Built in 1920 by Walter L. Barrows and designed by Harry Lewis, it hosted Benny Goodman, Cab Calloway, Guy Lombardo, Paul Whiteman, as well as singers Rudy Vallee and Alice Fay. On summer evenings, well dressed people came from miles around to enjoy the music and dancing.

Photo plays were shown on the lower floor during the week and after the summer season, and local boys played basketball in the ballroom. Before the pavilion burned in 1933, residents used it for high school proms, Kiwanis ladies' nights, and other social functions. Photographs and information courtesy of the Bourne Town Archives

The Golf Club House, Hyannisport, in the 1920s. Photograph courtesy of the Trayser Museum

Golf Club House, HYANNISPORT, Mass.

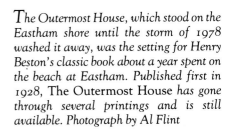

The Outermost House, which stood on the Eastham shore until the storm of 1978 washed it away, was the setting for Henry Beston's classic book about a year spent on the beach at Eastham. Published first in 1928, The Outermost House has gone through several printings and is still available. Photograph by Al Flint

The first Massachusetts woman legislator was Sylvia Donaldson, who was born and brought up in Falmouth. She was a school principal in Brockton before serving in the Massachusetts House of Representatives, beginning January 3, 1923. Photograph courtesy of the Falmouth Historical Society

Indians took pride in their heritage. Here are Mashpee Indians pictured in front of the Old Indian Church in 1923. They are (left to right): Chief Nelson Simons, Priscilla Pells, Mrs. Dorcas Gardner (Mashpee postmistress), Mrs. Elizabeth Coombs (sitting), Eben Wueppish, Mrs. Anna Pocknett, Charles Peters, Mrs. Sarah Pocknett (daughter of Blind Joe Amos), Mrs. Martha Edwards and daughter Selena Edwards, Cyrus Edwards (master carpenter), William Simons (uncle of the chief). One person is unidentified. Photograph from the Lombard Collection, Bourne Historical Society; courtesy of the Bourne Town Archives

The last of the hurdy gurdy grinders that entertained Cape Codders as it was trundled from village to village is shown here by Carl Bolles in 1930. Photograph from the Bourne Historical Society Collection; courtesy of the Bourne Town Archives

*J*oan Allen McNaughton enjoying a swing. *Photograph courtesy of Joan Allen MacNaughton*

*S*ports began to develop to a greater degree in schools. Here is the Barnstable High School baseball team of 1930. Photograph courtesy of John Howland Crocker

Barnstable High School football team in 1931. John Howland Crocker, right guard, is in the front row, third from the left. Photograph courtesy of John Howland Crocker

Before churches had youth organizations with national connections, there were local groups who met religious and social purposes. Here is the Scrooby Club of the South Congregational Church, Centerville, taken in the 1930s.

Back row (left to right): Lawrence Lovequist, Barry Weigert, Merle Lane, *Russell Starck, William Ruska, Oscar O. Johnson, Harry F. Johnson, Leo Ruska.*

Third row: Thelma Johnson (Brown), Frances Gardner, Betty Hazelton (Semprini), Violet Siira (Nickerson), Stephen Fuller, Ruth Lovequist (Littlefield), Inga Starck.

Second row: Jean McKenzie (Bearse), *Dorothy Siira (Kittila), Dagmar Flinkman, Reverend Philo G. Noon, Barbara Bearse, Dorothy Scallan.*

Front row: John Bleicken, Barbara Siira, Mildred Cole (White), Agnes Weigert, Elizabeth Gardner, Gladys Phillips, Elsa Starck, Elna Ruska (Nelson). Photograph courtesy of Barbara Bearse

On the grounds of the Cape Playhouse in Dennis is the Cape Cinema, which is famed for its gigantic mural by Rockwell Kent. The world-renowned artist collaborated with scenic artist Jo Mielziner to produce "the largest single canvas in the world. . . . It is 6400 square feet and is the artist's conception of heaven," according to Evelyn Lawson in her book Theater on Cape Cod.

The section pictured here features the dominant figure of the bull. The mural contains comets, constellations, and the hazy Milky Way.

This gem of a movie house was designed by New York architect Alfred Easton Poor and built in 1930. Photograph courtesy of the Cape Playhouse

Harvesting ice was an important activity until the days of refrigeration. This series of pictures shows the ice blocks being cut and guided into the trough that would eventually, via pulley, guide them into the icehouse. Some of the last of this activity took place in the 1930s as is shown here on Sandy Pond in West Yarmouth. Photographs courtesy of Tales of Cape Cod, Inc.

This icehouse was built for Boston Merchant Samuel Hooper on his Cotuit estate in 1850. It later became a study for Professor James Hardy Ropes and is now owned by Edward J. L. Ropes. Photograph courtesy of Patricia Anderson and Harriet Ropes Cabot

*O*pera star Lily Pons and conductor Andre Kostelanetz on their honeymoon at Oyster Harbors in Barnstable in 1939. Photograph by Percy Williams

*G*reat festivities occurred during the tercentenary of the town of Sandwich in 1939. (Though it was settled in 1637, it was not incorporated until 1639.)

Thornton W. Burgess, native-born author, is shown speaking at the anniversary meeting, which was held in front of the Casino, a building used for public meetings, social events, graduations, and even roller skating. Photograph courtesy of the Sandwich Town Archives

The 1939 tercentenary parade. This coach, driven by Henry Snow and loaned by the restaurant Hell's Blazes, is shown passing the corner of Liberty Street and Route 6A. Photograph courtesy of the Sandwich Town Archives

Barnstable also celebrated a tercentenary in 1939. One of the highlights was the placing of twelve memorial tablets with appropriate dedication ceremonies.

On Sunday, July 30, Elisha B. Worrell of Boston and Centerville delivered the dedication address for the marker in memory of the first settlers of Centerville, known earlier as Chequaquet. Two newly planted English beech trees flanked the stone.

Each of the villages celebrated on a special week, and the united churches gave a tercentenary pageant. Photograph from Proceedings of the Tercentenary Anniversary of Barnstable, Massachusetts

Mayor Charles Dart and the Mayoress of Barnstaple, England, came as emissaries from the namesake town in Devon. Arriving August 12, they were welcomed by town officials and honored at a reception and dinner at the Wianno Club. They are shown here with High Sheriff Lauchlan M. Crocker at the opening of the Tercentenary Fair. Photograph from Proceedings of the Tercentenary Anniversary of Barnstable, Massachusetts

Actress Gertrude Lawrence with her husband theatrical producer Richard Aldrich in Dennis, August 1952. Photograph by Richard C. Kelsey; courtesy of Percy Williams

Chapter 11

Maturity

1941-1960

In 1939 the guns of Europe boomed again. Dark war clouds formed over more and more countries. News continually worsened as the conflagration spread. When the Japanese attacked Pearl Harbor on December 7, 1941, the United States declared war.

Cape Codders stepped in immediately to play their part. As in the First World War, the theater of action was overseas, but preparations for the defense of the homeland proceeded. There were dimouts and blackouts, particularly along the coast and by the entrances to the Cape Cod Canal, where enemy submarines lay in wait. Warships picked up their merchant counterparts on either side of the canal to convoy them across the Atlantic.

Early in the 1920s, the Field Artillery of the twenty-sixth Division of the National Guard maintained a tent camp on the eastern side of the canal. Later it was named Camp Edwards for General Clarence R. Edwards, commander of the twenty-sixth Division during World War I.

A small airfield, hewn from scrub pine and underbrush at Camp Edwards had been officially named for Lieutenant Frank Otis, a Massachusetts National Guard pilot, 101st Observation, who was killed in a plane crash while on maneuvers. During World War II, the fourteenth Anti-Submarine Patrol flew daily patrols in search of these German U-boats that menaced shipping. Though dormant for a period, in 1949 the airfield became Otis Air Force Base.

The *U.S.S. Barnstable*, named for the county, was an attack transport that saw much activity in the Pacific. Other local vessels which had once carried passengers to Martha's Vineyard and Nantucket took part in the Normandy invasion and ferried supplies and men regularly across the English Channel.

At home amphibious teams trained on the beaches. Coast Guard service was increased. Cape Codders enlisted in all service branches, many serving in the navy and merchant marine because of their abilities as seamen. These included women, who were WACS, WAVES, SPARS, and Marines.

Church groups and fraternal organizations tried valiantly to raise the spirits of the public and the service personnel on nearby posts. They coped with lessening food and fuel under rationing. In spite of this there were tensions caused by rumors of spies and heightened by the torpedoing of a ship off Provincetown in 1943. Although Civil Defense units Cape-wide rushed to aid the stricken vessel, only half of the passengers and crew were rescued.

The Cape was now into the air age. Though the first airplane had landed on an old race track in Hyannis in 1928, the town had not purchased the fledgling field until 1936. During the Second World War, the United States Navy took it over and improved it considerably. When the military turned over the Barnstable Airport to the town, the field immediately became commercially important. Ironically, about the time the last of the passenger trains rode down the Cape's iron rails, the first of the passenger planes took to the air.

Then Germany fell in May 1945 and Japan surrendered that September. The war had lasted six long years and a day. It had involved twenty-seven nations and caused appalling human and material devastation. Equally as grave, the bombs falling on Hiroshima and Nagasaki had ushered in the age of the atom with all its promise and potential doom. Cape Codders rejoiced with those who had survived and mourned over those who had not.

Once again residents turned their energies to rebuilding a war-torn economy. Business leaders looked first to the resort industry, but they realized this brought income only in the warm months. So, encouraged by the increasing number of retirees country-wide, officials laid plans to attract more of these as year-round residents. Gray-haired residents would provide regular income for local businesses they reasoned, while the vacationers who arrived with the spring robins and continued through the golden days of Indian summer, would bring the extra money. Furthermore, this age resident would not require more schools!

Many over sixty-fivers, attracted by the less frantic pace and the rustic seaside charm which still remained in many villages, moved across the bridges. They found golf courses playable most of the year; many fraternal, cultural, and social organizations; a varied horticulture that included even a holly belt; and (most of the time) milder winters. Almost overnight a new community appeared on Cape Cod maps when the award-winning leisure villages of New Seabury were constructed on Mashpee shores.

The *Wonderful Way of Life* booklet of the Cape Cod Chamber of Commerce made the Cape's advantages widely known. The unseen Lorelei was again casting its spell. Amusingly, once these new arrivals had put down their roots, they liked to put on the mantle of the natives. They crossed the bridges to the mainland only under dire necessity and they eyed newcomers askance.

Changes in transportation aided the influx. Rail passenger service, so vital in earlier years, had its last run in 1959. But the automobile and the superhighway ribbons unrolling across the country brought the masses. Regularly scheduled buses connected New York and Boston with Hyannis, and air travel connected the Cape with the major cities of the world.

Communication became more sophisticated. Weekly newspapers had begun in the 1800s. The *Barnstable Patriot*, Cape Cod's oldest and one of the country's earliest, dates from 1830. The daily *Cape Cod Times* rolled off the presses first in 1936 and has developed into a major paper with the latest equipment. Eventually, in addition to the twice-weekly *Falmouth Enterprise* and the *Cape Codder*, there would be thirteen weeklies disseminating the news.

All the news was not distributed by print. The 1940s also saw the beginnings of radio when WOCB went on the air. After an intermittent start, WOCB-AM became a permanent fixture in 1944. An FM station (now with call letters WSOX) was added in 1947. Later these would be joined by four others (WCIB Falmouth, WCOD Hyannis, WQRC Hyannis, WKZE Orleans) as well as a subsidiary office of Plymouth's WPLM and later broadcasts from the Cape Cod Community College's WKKL and Provincetown's WOMR.

Though television was gathering its avid watchers, Cape Codders relied on off-Cape channels. They had to wait until the late 1960s before cable companies arrived to wire the towns, bring a stronger signal, and make community programming available. A television station came later.

The postwar years and the influx of retirees with both time and talent brought new life to the arts. The Cape Cod Art Association, founded in 1948, held classes and exhibitions in its Hyannis quarters, but was already looking forward to new and permanent headquarters. In July 1973 it was to move into the present modern-style building on Route 6A in Barnstable Village.

There were musicians and dancers who had retired to the Cape, so in 1956 the Cape Cod Conservatory of Music and Arts was born. It grew rapidly and moved several times during the next two decades until the new home was built on Route 132 in West Barnstable. Offices of the Cape Cod Symphony, founded in 1961, are also in this building.

Across the highway from the conservatory is another impressive modern-style complex, Cape Cod Community College. Established as the result of the Commonwealth's Community College Act of 1958, it was the third such in the state to be created. The first faculty was gathered in 1960, and classes began in September 1961. First temporary quarters were, quite fittingly, in one of the brick buildings that first housed the Hyannis Normal School of the last century.

Sports activity increased. Games had been played on this peninsula since the Indians and Pilgrims feasted and played for three days in the fall of 1621. To the tennis courts and golf courses that were constructed around the turn of the century were added baseball and football fields. These sports became integral parts of school activity along with basketball, hockey, and skating. The Cape Cod Baseball League, which dates to the 1920s, has spawned many a major league player including Thurmon Munson of the New York Yankees. Boxers trained and sparred.

In 1957 the Joseph P. Kennedy family, for many years summer residents of Hyannis Port, presented the town of Barnstable with the Kennedy Memorial Skating Rink in memory of Joseph P. Kennedy, Jr., whose plane crashed in World War II. Rinks and different recreational facilities would follow in Bourne, Falmouth, and other towns.

The Barnstable Municipal Airport, pictured here in 1938, is now a modern airfield with private and passenger service. In July 1981 John Polando of Sandwich and the late Russell Boardman were honored with ceremonies. On the fiftieth anniversary of their historic flight overseas, the field was named the Boardman-Polando Field. Photograph by Percy Williams

*T*en thousand people watched the Defense Day parade in Hyannis August 31, 1941. Elmer A. E. Richards, chairman of the Defense Committee of the Hyannis Lodge of Elks (sponsor organization), was head of the event.

Selectman James F. Kenney headed the parade, followed by Wampanoag Indians, then Virginia Lawes and Eleanor Richards carrying the theme banner.

Over sixty floats, twelve bands, a Cape drum and bugle corps, scouts, Camp Fire Girls, and all branches of the service were represented in the mile-long parade which took two-and-a-half hours to pass the reviewing stand on Main Street. Photograph courtesy of Elmer A. E. Richards

The oldest steam fire engine on Cape Cod was in the Defense Day parade August 31, 1941. Charles Clagg was driving; Ralph Chamberlain, a House of Correction guard, stood by. Photograph courtesy of the Trayser Museum

United States Congressman Charles L. Gifford (left), pictured here in 1940 with actress Gertrude Lawrence and Henry L. Davis of Bass River, was the speaker at the Defense Day parade in Hyannis August 31, 1941. Gifford told the huge crowd assembled at the Barnstable High School Athletic Field after the parade that Cape Cod leads the state and the state leads the nation in civil defense, according to the September 2 issue of the Cape Cod Standard Times.

A Cotuit resident, Gifford was a member of the state House of Representatives in 1912 and 1913 and, the state Senate from 1914 to 1919, he filled a vacancy to the Sixty-Seventh Congress and was reelected to eleven succeeding Congresses, remaining until his death in 1947. Photograph by Frederick Miller, Jr.; courtesy of Percy Williams

Members of the Massachusetts Army National Guard's 101st Engineer Battalion arrived at Camp Edwards in June 1941. Troops who trained here left for the Pacific and Europe when Pearl Harbor was bombed in December 1941. New recruits from the Cape and elsewhere quickly took their places. Photograph courtesy of the Department of the Army, Camp Edwards Headquarters

The USS Barnstable, *named for the county, was an attack transport involved in a number of the landings in the Pacific theater of war during World War II. Photograph courtesy of the Cape Cod Times*

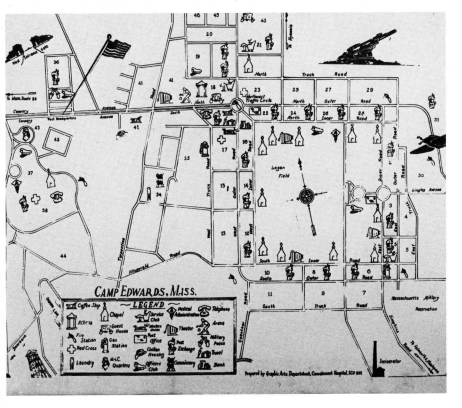

CAMP EDWARDS, MASS.

Camp Edwards, *birthplace of the Amphibian Engineers. Photograph from* Down Ramp *by Brigadier General William F. Heavey*

Soldiers practice amphibious landings on a Cape Cod beach. Photograph from Down Ramp by Brigadier General William F. Heavey

Shore engineers install markers and prepare a road for troops to practice landing on a Cape Cod beach. Photograph from Down Ramp by Brigadier General William F. Heavey

Tales of Cape Cod, Inc. was founded in 1949 to record the voices of old-time Cape Codders recalling what it was like many years before. Louis Cataldo (left), the first president, is shown recording the words of Clara Jane Hallett of Hyannis who reached 100 years of age and who for many years was a columnist for the Barnstable Patriot. Dorothy Worrell, vice-president, (right) assisted Cataldo in founding the Cape-wide historical organization when she was editor of the Barnstable Patriot.

Recordings are still being made, and copies are placed in the Cape Cod room of the Library Learning Resource Center at the Cape Cod Community College. The public may listen to these by prior arrangement with the college audio visual department. This photograph was taken on September 19, 1955, on the occasion of Miss Hallett's ninety-seventh birthday. Photograph courtesy of Tales of Cape Cod, Inc.

Sports announcers Mel Allen (second from left) and New York Yankee player Phil Rizzuto (far right) at an awards ceremony of the Cape Cod Baseball League in 1954. Photograph by Percy Williams

Chatham artist Alice Stallknecht depicted many of her neighbors in religious scenes such as Christ Preaching to the Multitude and The Circle Supper. Later she used her neighbors in the mural Everyman To His Trade, as depicted here.

The subject of much controversy, her murals were first placed in the First Congregational Church of Chatham, then stored in a shed. After her death in 1973, the murals were restored and can now be seen during the summer at the Chatham Historical Society. Photograph by Stuart Eyman

The Blessing of the Fleet ceremony held in Provincetown the last Sunday in June is a fiesta as well as a religious observance. After the Fisherman's Mass in St. Peter's Church, the bishop of the diocese blesses each boat as it passes in review in the harbor. Begun in 1948, the ceremony is a reminder of the Portuguese heritage. Photograph courtesy of the Cape Cod Chamber of Commerce and the Massachusetts Department of Commerce

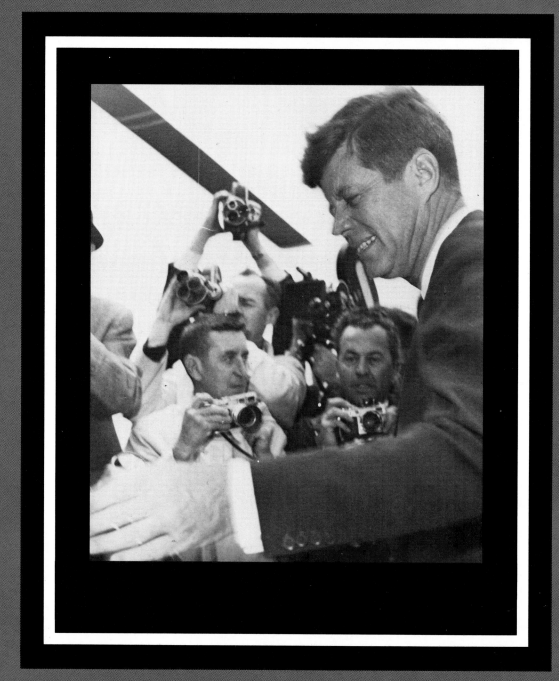

John F. Kennedy arrived at Barnstable Airport after his nomination for the presidency on the Democratic ticket the summer of 1960. Photograph by Percy Williams

Chapter 12

New
Consciousness

1961-1982

With the dawning of the 1960s a sunburst of activity flamed in the arts, sports, churches, business, social services, clubs, and politics.

Participants in the Cape Cod Writers' Conference joined the multifaceted art scene when the first session was held in 1963 at the Craigville Conference Center. Now in its twentieth year, the conference enables writers and would-be writers to sharpen skills, share experiences, and rub shoulders with professionals in the publishing world each August. In addition, the organization cooperates with school representatives in the Writers-in-the-Schools program.

There are presently some 150 authors who live or summer on this peninsula, drawn by the peacefulness which encourages productivity and by the closeness to agents and publishers in New York and Boston. Kurt Vonnegut, Jr., Jacques Barzun, Monica Dickens, Marge Piercy, and Paul Theroux are but a few of the major writers with Cape Cod connections.

Sports became even more diversified with the arrival of bowling leagues, racquetball clubs, curling, and even a Cape Cod ski club (whose members most often have to journey elsewhere for their fun). Major sports events, as well as entertainment, can be showcased in the Cape Cod Coliseum in Yarmouth.

Churches increased in size, number, and building additions during these turbulent years until now there are close to 140 religious societies representing more than thirty denominations. Realizing that many human needs can be met better by working together rather than alone, religious leaders founded the Cape Cod Council of Churches in 1967. Today the council coordinates pastoral counseling services, chaplaincy programs in the jail and hospitals, as well as a clothing depot and thrift shop.

Civic associations and boards of trade had emerged in the various villages and towns to encourage and watch business activity. The smaller family-run stores gradually gave way to supermarket chains and shopping malls. In the late 1960s, the enclosed Cape Cod Mall and the Capetown Plaza were built on Route 132 in Hyannis, followed by the enclosed Falmouth Mall. Smaller shopping plazas began to dot the Cape. Industrial parks were begun in Hyannis (Independence Park), Sandwich, and Falmouth. Small industry like Augat in Mashpee and Packaging Industries of Hyannis added to job stability. Banks, which began with the Falmouth National in 1821, have now proliferated to about seventeen, many with a multiplicity of branches.

The 1980 census revealed a population of 147,925 residents, so more services were required by towns and social service agencies. So many of these people were elderly that Elder Services of Cape Cod and the Islands came into being, and residential retirement homes were established to augment existing nursing facilities. Most towns assisted the lower income elderly with housing, and churches sought to alleviate housing needs of moderate-income elderly and families. The Barnstable Association United Church of Christ, consisting of twenty Congregational (United Church of Christ) churches, sponsors six such housing facilities.

The Cape Cod Hospital had meanwhile grown into a multi-million-dollar complex with the finest equipment, including the latest for cancer treatment. Outreach centers in Wellfleet and Harwich assist residents in the Lower Cape, and the Barnstable County Hospital in Pocasset and the Falmouth Hospital provide care in the Upper Cape. These staffs, aided by paramedics and town medical units, cope nobly with the increasing problems that arrive with the annual summer influx.

Social service organizations have proliferated. According to the Cape Cod Community Council, there are approximately 200 agencies, organizations, and support groups endeavoring to meet the myriad human needs. In 1980 Volunteers of Cape Cod, Inc. was organized to coordinate and channel volunteer aid.

The Vietnam War, along with the earlier strife in Korea, involved Cape men and women. Though the impact on local economy was not great, the toll of the heartstrings was considerable. The split in public opinion over the latter war particularly, and the loss of life, brought untold anguish. Memorial markers to the valiant ones who gave their lives have been placed in towns and villages.

The tremendous explosion of people and programs brought ecological concerns to the forefront. People voiced their apprehension that dune buggies were destroying the fragile beach grasses, necessary to hold down the sand dunes. Others asked how many buildings should be allowed on the land when there is a diminishing water supply. The clamor of voices with ecological concerns rose in crescendo. Problems of uncertain water resources, erosion of seaside charm, disposal of solid waste, inadequate housing, and spot zoning hit the fifteen towns.

One of the happier results of this growing ecological concern was the creation of the Cape Cod National Seashore Park. Established by Congress in 1961 with headquarters at Eastham, the 27,000-acre park along the Atlantic shore was dedicated in 1966. Circling terns, wild flowers, beach grass, and fragile dunes were saved from snorting bulldozers, preserved for young and old for all time.

One of those instrumental in creating this park was the charismatic senator from Massachusetts, John Fitzgerald Kennedy. When Kennedy won the presidential election and was sworn in January 1961, the political scene on the Cape went into high gear. In earlier centuries the Cape was known around the globe because its sea captains traded in the world's exotic ports. Now Cape Cod was famous the world over as the location of the Kennedy Compound and the summer White House.

Kennedy, his charming wife Jacqueline, and children Caroline and John captured the fancy of the media, the country, and the world. The parents of the president and their progeny had always been in the news. The multimillionaire patriarch Joseph P. Kennedy, businessman with acumen and former ambassador to England, and his wife Rose, devout mother of nine, had always been public spirited. The president's brothers—Robert, first the U. S. Attorney General and later a senator from New York, and Edward, senator from Massachusetts—were constantly in the news.

Tourists poured onto the Cape in ever-increasing numbers asking the perennial question, "Where is the Kennedy Compound?" They still come and they still ask, even though President Kennedy's life was so tragically ended by an assassin's bullet in Texas on November 22, 1963, and his brother Robert was similarly killed in California in June 1968. Senator Edward Kennedy is now the head of the family and a dynamic figure in American politics.

Ecological concerns still simmer, but answers are beginning to surface. A mark of a mature people has always been the willingness to face problems squarely and make the hard decisions and sacrifices necessary for survival. Fortunately Cape Codders have entered the current arena armed with an aroused public and concerned leadership. They also have a long heritage of tenacity to aid in coping with the Cape's vulnerability.

In an economic recession, citizens of all ages are developing alternate ways of earning a living, from contemporary crafts to small industries. Less costly energy is being found with solar panels and a return to the windmill concept of earlier days. The award-winning Ecology House in Marstons Mills demonstrates that folk can live on the land unobtrusively and economically. Geodesic domes and fish vats at the New Alchemy Institute in Hatchville point to better ways of living, working, and producing food.

The Cape Cod Planning and Economic Development Commission has urged county-wide action on common problems and reminds developers to perpetuate the village greens, so long associated with Cape tradition. The Association for the Preservation of Cape Cod was chartered to educate and coordinate citizen action. Ecology-minded organizations like the Cape Cod Museum of Natural History in Brewster are raising the consciousness of all age groups.

This new consciousness, now at an all-time high, has brought us full circle. The native Americans who dwelt on this land before Europeans arrived have always been ecologically oriented. The League of the Haudenosaunee (or Six Nation Iroquois Confederacy), which has been functioning continuously for 1,000 years in North America, has always emphasized the responsibility of all for seven generations into the future.

There are whispered legends that fabulous riches lie undiscovered under Cape Cod sands, buried long ago by pirates. But both natives and later comers now know that this unique peninsula is a much greater treasure than all the scintillating jewels and golden doubloons in a pirate's treasure trove.

The Kennedy Compound as seen from the air shows the home of the late Ambassador Kennedy in the left foreground with the flagpole; the home of the late Senator Robert Kennedy to the left; and the home of the late President John F. Kennedy directly behind the covered swimming pool in back of the ambassador's home. Photographs copyright Julius Lazarus, Hyannis, Massachusetts

Home Of The Late Senator Robert F. Kennedy

Home Of The Late President John F Kennedy

Home Of The Late Ambassador Joseph P. Kennedy

President John Fitzgerald Kennedy at a press conference in Washington, D.C. Photograph courtesy of the John F. Kennedy Library

President Kennedy and his small son John are shown arriving at Otis Air Force Base. From here, they helicoptered to the Kennedy Compound in Hyannis Port. Photograph courtesy of the John F. Kennedy Library

The young president relaxing aboard his Wianno Senior, the Victura, in the waters off Hyannis Port. Photograph courtesy of the John F. Kennedy Library

Falmouth Hospital with its helicopter pad in the lower left and Bramblebush Medical Complex at right. The hospital opened in May 1963. Photograph by Hugo Poisson; courtesy of Falmouth Hospital

The Coast Guard helicopter and staff bringing a patient to the Falmouth Hospital. Photograph by Hugo Poisson; courtesy of Falmouth Hospital

Tales of Cape Cod, Inc., which owns the seven-and-a-half-acre site in Cummaquid where the remains of Indian Chief Iyanough were discovered in 1861, has offered the area for reburial of any Indian remain found on the Cape. Here Reverend Peter Palches (left) officiates at a reburial on August 12, 1964. Others in the foreground are (left to right): selectman Thomas Murphy, president Louis Cataldo, vice-president Dorothy Worrell, and director Keith Bunting. William Covell (left) and George Blaney in background. Photograph courtesy of Tales of Cape Cod, Inc.

A whale ninety feet long washed up on the shore near Corporation Beach in Dennis in the early 1970s. This is not an uncommon event on the Cape, but it always draws a crowd. In early days all drift whales became property of the town parson, but after a few days the whales became very smelly and there is no record of a parson claiming his prize. Photograph courtesy of the Historical Society of Old Yarmouth

International friendship was epitomized when Reverend Peter and Lois Palches (left) hosted Russian sailors from the research vessel Albatross November 1, 1967. The sailors (left to right), Herman Camopogal, Pranos Pallickas, and Rudolph Draginy, were taken to the Kennedy Memorial in Hyannis while they were on leave from the ship docked at Woods Hole. Photograph courtesy of Lois and Peter Palches

*B*allet dancer Valerie Clarke tested a new pair of toe shoes before a performance of Cinderella at the Harwich High School, August 1969. Photograph by Dick Holbrook

*G*olden wedding celebrations are much more frequent on the Cape now that people are living longer and more retirees are moving here. In June 1972 family and friends of Reverend Paul and Mrs. Evelyn Johnson (center couple with leis) gathered to celebrate their fiftieth anniversary at Weathervane Pond.

Reverend Peter (left) and Mrs. Lois Palches (third left of Mrs. Johnson) were hosts to Mrs. Palches' sister-in-law and husband's celebration. Reverend Paul Schilling (right with camera) and his wife Mary (in front of him) were Osterville neighbors; Reverend Roy and Mrs. Ruth Colby (far right) were formerly of Osterville where Roy served the Osterville Methodist Church. Photograph by R. Taylor Drake; courtesy of Lois Johnson Cummings

*C*raigville Inn on the Green, the 110-year-old conference center's largest building, has thirty guest rooms and a large dining room overlooking Red Lily Pond. Photograph by Marion Vuilleumier

The Craigville Conference Center of the Christian Camp Meeting Association celebrated its 100th birthday in 1972. At the banquet, the highlight of centennial week, these dignitaries gathered: (left to right) Reverend Dr. Myron Fowell, secretary of Massachusetts Conference, United Church of Christ; the late Reverend Dr. Pierre DuPont Vuilleumier, director of Craigville Conference Center and Southeastern Area minister for the U.C.C.; the Honorable Edward Brooke, former United States senator from Massachusetts; the late James Buffington, president of the Christian Camp Meeting Association; Thomas Murphy, selectman of the town of Barnstable. Photograph by Howard Studios; courtesy of the Craigville Conference Center

Some of the thirty-two restored antique motor cars on display at Heritage Plantation of Sandwich. These may be seen in a two-story round stone barn a replica of an unusual Shaker barn design from early nineteenth century America. Photograph courtesy of the Cape Cod Chamber of Commerce

Chief Mittark (Lorenzo Jeffers) of Martha's Vineyard and Waquoit, who until his death on July 23, 1974, was supreme sachem of the Wampanoags, the position held by Massasoit when the Pilgrims came.

Chief Mittark was descended from the original Mittark who sold parts of Martha's Vineyard to the settlers and is mentioned in Some Pious Indian Chiefs. He attended the Indian school in Carlisle, Pennsylvania, and worked with the tribes to promote the consciousness of the Indian heritage. Photograph by Pierre DuPont Vuilleumier

The Operations Center of Sentry Co-operative Bank, which was built in 1975 in Independence Park in Hyannis, is quite a contrast from the Cape's first bank, housed in a small cottage on Falmouth's Main Street in 1821. This modern building holds the computers and data necessary for the operation of the bank's thirteen branches. Photograph from Craig Studio; courtesy of Sentry Cooperative Bank

The Cape Cod Community College complex, which is strategically located at the intersection of routes 6 and 132, is a two-year, fully accredited school which offers courses for students of all ages. Construction of the impressive plan began in 1966, and it was finally completed in 1976. Photograph courtesy of the Cape Cod Community College Library

The interior of the four-story Library Learning Resource Center at the Cape Cod Community College can accommodate 50,000 volumes. It has 375 student carrels, an audio-visual resource center, and a forty-two-place language laboratory.

A very special feature is its collection of Cape Cod materials. In the William Brewster Nickerson Room of Cape Cod History and Literature, there are books, magazines, clippings, deeds, etc., that relate to Cape Cod and its people. Books by Cape authors or about Cape subjects are collected, and college officials welcome such gifts. This special room is staffed by volunteers, some of whom have given their time since the college library opened. Many come through the Retired Senior Volunteer Program. Charlotte Price, a professional archivist, works in the room two days a week through a grant from the Edward Bangs Kelley and Elza Kelley Foundation. Photograph by Samuels Studio; courtesy of the Cape Cod Community College Library

Author Catherine Woolley (left) of Truro, who also writes as Jane Thayer, is shown with Geraldine Gill, elementary school librarian for the town of Barnstable, at one of the Writers-in-the-Schools programs. They are admiring Gus, a character from Gus The Friendly Ghost, one of Miss Woolley's many children's books. The Cape Cod Writers' Conference works with school officials to arrange these programs in many schools. This author appeared in the Marstons Mills Elementary School in February 1980. Photograph by Marion Vuilleumier

Henry Fonda and Myrna Loy were pictured while filming Summer Solstice, a television movie at Pamet Beach in Truro in the fall of 1980. Photograph by Stuart Eyman

The tiniest craft to leave the Cape for Europe is pictured. French adventurer Gerard d'Abouville was snapped as he left Chatham July 10, 1980, for his Atlantic crossing. He and his specially constructed rowboat arrived in France September 20, 1980. Photograph by Stuart Eyman

The U.S.S. Cape Cod (AD 43) was launched August 2, 1980, at 3:45 p.m. at the National Shipbuilding Company, San Diego, California. The ship is a 642-foot destroyer tender which will provide a mobile base and maintenance support facilities for destroyers, cruisers, frigates, light patrol ships, and miscellaneous small craft. Seventeen of the crew of 1,400 enlisted persons and eighty-seven officers are from Cape Cod.

Through the efforts of retired petty officer Douglas Park of Wellfleet and Gladys Reed of Hyannis, money has been raised to provide the traditional gift of a silver service to the ship.

Robert J. Murray, former undersecretary of the navy spoke at the launching, and his wife Betty christened the bow with champagne. Their daughter Victoria Ann Murray of Orleans was maid of honor.

Recruits are Edward Moore of Bourne; Michael Challies of Brewster; John Sanna of Buzzards Bay; Heidi Hergesheimer of Chatham; Penny Peterson and Candace Robichau of Dennis; Christopher Greim of Eastham; Roseann Scruggs of Falmouth; Scott Britton and Joseph Cataloni of Har-

wich; Kathleen Ricketts of Oak Bluffs (Martha's Vineyard); Stephan Lenart and David Pell of Sandwich; Gregory Lavalle and Charles Small of Wareham; Brian Moran of Wellfleet; Richard Philbrook of Yarmouth. Captain Robert F. Baril (USN) is the commanding officer.

There was an early Cape Cod—a freighter converted to a troopship during World War II. From 1943 to 1946 the vessel transported troops in the Pacific, then was released. Photograph courtesy of the National Steel and Shipbuilding Company

At the first annual Awards Banquet of the NAACP in April 1982 in Hyannis, Joseph DaLuz (center) president of the Cape Cod branch presented an award to Margaret and Emerson Mosley (left). Benjamin Hook, director of the National Association (seated) was with Frank Rhodes (standing), vice-president of the Cape Cod branch.

Awards are presented to people who have given an extra measure to the development of human resources, especially on behalf of blacks and other minorities. Photograph by Dolores DaLuz

Reverend George Jaques of Marstons Mills is shown feeding goats that soon will be off to some needy area in the world through the Heifer Project. Jaques has been instrumental in raising funds and people's consciousness of this worthy program which gives "a hand instead of a handout." Recipients of goats will promise to give the first-born offspring to another needy family. Photograph by Lou LaPrade

Directors and volunteers of the Retired Senior Volunteer Program gathered at the State House in Boston when Governor Edward King signed a proclamation recognizing the services of RSVP volunteers in Massachusetts August 17, 1981.

Participants were (left to right): Kathleen Dash, state program specialist; Arevaloif Kasparian, Lawrence volunteer; Yvonne Drauschke, Lawrence director; Joan Thompson, Plymouth director; Ross Parkam, project director from Somerville; Freddie Jackson, former project director for Springfield; Arnold Sammuels, Springfield volunteer; Don Wright, ACTION state program director; Leighton Harris, board of directors, Cape Cod RSVP from Chatham; Florence Myles, Somerville volunteer; Harry Webb, state program specialist; Agnes Harris of Chatham, volunteer at Cape Cod RSVP.

Volunteers of Cape Cod, Inc. is the sponsor for RSVP, Younger Volunteer, and the Inside/Out program for homebound volunteers on Cape Cod. Through its efforts in recruiting and placing volunteers, many human service organizations receive countless hours of volunteer time. Photograph courtesy of Volunteers of Cape Cod, Inc.

Woods Hole from the air showing the ferry to the Islands (left), Woods Hole Oceanographic Institution (center), the Marine Biological Laboratory on Eel Pond (right) with the National Marine Fisheries Service behind it. Photograph courtesy of Woods Hole Oceanographic Institution

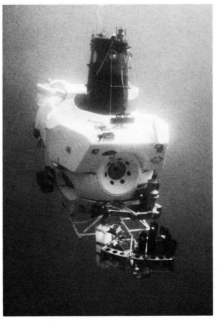

The submersible Alvin is operated by the Woods Hole Oceanographic Institution for the American oceanographic research community. The sub takes a pilot and two scientific observers to depths of 4,000 meters for sampling, photography, and observation in the deep ocean. Photograph by John Porteous; courtesy of the Woods Hole Oceanographic Institution

The Media Balloon Race is held annually to benefit the Doreen Grace Center for Brain Research, which is being established in New Seabury. Photograph by Eric Michelsen

The submersible Alvin, *pictured with its mother ship* Lulu. *Photograph by Larry Shumaker; courtesy of the Woods Hole Oceanographic Institution*

This *photo shows the Cape Cod Hospital with Whitcomb Pavilion in the foreground, the cranberry bogs owned by the hospital to the right, and the main building top center. Hyannis Harbor is in the foreground, and Lewis Bay Convalescent Home (not hospital-connected) is at left. Photograph by Richard Kelsey; courtesy of Cape Cod Hospital*

Artists *have flocked to Provincetown since Charles W. Hawthorne, famed portrait painter, started the Cape Cod School of Art. Since then art associations have sprung into being throughout the peninsula, and outdoor art shows like the one above in Orleans abound in summer. Photograph courtesy of the Cape Cod Chamber of Commerce*

Oil painting class in the studio of the Falmouth Artists' Guild, which was formed in 1966 and now has a membership of over 400 artists, craftsmen, teachers, business people, and friends. Housed in the Peter Yost Public House, former Falmouth "poor farm," the guild offers continuous exhibitions of many art forms.

Left to right: Jeanne Herbert, Dante Memmolo, Mary O'Brien, John Benn, Eleanor Schley, and instructor Jean Ward. Photograph by William Morrison; courtesy of the Falmouth Artist's Guild

The Cape Cod Art Association sponsors outdoor shows as well as many exhibits inside its modern headquarters on Route 6A in Barnstable Village. Photograph by Nathaniel H. Pulling; courtesy of the Cape Cod Art Association

Arturo Viranto of Wellfleet, novelist and poet, is shown teaching the fiction class at the 1981 Cape Cod Writers' Conference. Photograph by Dick Holbrook; courtesy of the Cape Cod Writers' Conference

The Outermost House cup plate launched the annual series of literary cup plates in 1981. The book The Outermost House was written by Henry Beston when he remained in that Eastham building (now destroyed by a storm). The cup plate was designed by Cummaquid artist Louis Vuilleumier, engraved by Alvin White of Sandwich, and produced by the Pairpoint Glass Company of Sagamore. It represents over 150 designs from that company which are collected with fervor by enthusiasts.

The Thornton Burgess Society in Sandwich began the cup plate mania with delightful representations of Thornton Burgess's characters like Reddy Fox, Sammy Jay, Peter Rabbit, and Hooty the Owl.

Cup plates were created in England about 1810. First made of China, they were later created of glass by the Boston and Sandwich Glass Company and are now collectors items. When the art was revived in recent years by Pairpoint Company, a national organization sprang into being, the Pairpoint Cup Plate Collectors of America, and a new item was added to the already large group of collectibles. Photograph by Dick Holbrook; courtesy of the Cape Cod Writers' Conference

Kurt Vonnegut, Jr., formerly of Barnstable, autographed one of his novels for Harold Wilson, Jr., author and chairman of the 1968 conference at which Vonnegut lectured. Photograph by the Howard Studios; courtesy of the Cape Cod Writers' Conference

Barbara Witham (left) of West Yarmouth and other conferees are shown leaving the Craigville Tabernacle after a 1980 session of the annual August Cape Cod Writers' Conference. Photograph by Dick Holbrook; courtesy of the Cape Cod Writers' Conference

Author Monica Dickens of North Falmouth, great-granddaughter of Charles Dickens, is shown with her husband Commander Roy Stratton, who is also an author. The couple attended one of the receptions that opened an early Cape Cod Writers' Conference. Photograph courtesy of Commander Roy Stratton

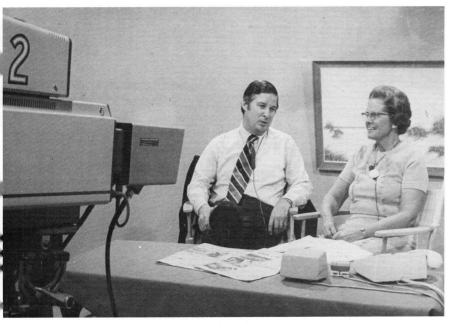

John Hughes, director of the Voice of America and former editor of the Christian Science Monitor, was a guest on the television show "Books and the World." The thirty-minute interview weekly program is a production of the Cape Cod Writers' Conference, and its executive secretary Marion Vuilleumier is the show host. Hughes is a resident of Orleans, and he and his wife Libby own Hughes Newspapers on the Cape. Photograph by Dick Holbrook; courtesy of the Cape Cod Writers' Conference

Cape Cod Conservatory of Music and Arts; Beebe Woods Art Center in Falmouth. Photograph courtesy of Cape Cod Conservatory of Music and Arts

A montage of activities at the Cape Cod Conservatory of Music and Arts in West Barnstable includes (upper left) a ballet class; (upper right) director Richard Casper with opera producer Sarah Caldwell; (center left to right) Willem Valkenier, retired Boston Symphony French horn player; artist Edwin Dickinson; Maureen Enos teaching an Orth class; Ernest White in front of the "Cape Cod Wall" of contributors; (lower left) an art class; (lower right) the late Arthur Fiedler with director Casper planning the Boston Pops concert on the Cape. Photographs of the Cape Cod Conservatory of Music and Arts

Jazz, an American form of music, is popular on Cape Cod. Marie Marcus, jazz pianist, was honored in March 1982 for her fifty-year career. A student of Fats Waller, she soon collected her own band and has played in all the major big-time jazz spots. Since the mid-1960s she has played regularly on Cape Cod, currently at the Columns in West Dennis. Other jazz greats with Cape connections are Dave McKenna, Lou Columbo, and the late Bobby Hackett. Photograph by John Rega

Cape Cod Symphony Orchestra, Royston Nash, conductor; May 1981. Photograph courtesy of the Cape Cod Symphony Orchestra Association, Inc.

Royston Nash was formerly with the D'Oyly Carte Opera Company in London. Photograph courtesy of the Cape Cod Symphony Orchestra Association, Inc.

213

Though passenger train travel ceased some time ago from points off Cape, an excursion train is now reviving train travel locally. The summer of 1981 saw the beginnings of the Cape Cod and Hyannis Scenic Railroad, which took passengers from Hyannis to Sandwich. In 1982 Mark Snider, the company president, is running his 350-passenger trains to Falmouth and Buzzards Bay in addition to Sandwich. Photograph by Marion Vuilleumier

Senator Edward M. Kennedy spoke to elderly citizens at the hot lunch program at the Old Colony Apartments, town of Barnstable in Hyannis January 1982. The nutrition program is part of Elder Services of Cape Cod and the Islands in which close to 500 volunteers provide meals not only in center like this, but also to the homebound through Meals on Wheels.

Senator Kennedy is a resident of the town and votes in its Precinct 3 South. Photograph by Gordon Caldwell; courtesy of the Elder Service Nutrition Program

Charlotte Price, archivist, and Dudley Hallett, president, at the Falmouth Historical Society. Mrs. Price, former archivist at the Pilgrim Society in Plymouth, now works at the Bourne Archives, the Woods Hole Historical Collection, and the Cape Cod Community College as well as at the Falmouth Historical Society. She is guiding these organizations in the filing and the protection of their historical materials. Mr. Hallett represents the many retirees who give countless hours to historical societies. Photograph by Marion Vuilleumier

Members of the Nye family at the 1981 reunion in front of the Nye homestead in Sandwich. Benjamin Nye built the old home in 1685 and ran a fulling mill nearby. He was also supervisor of highways and operated a sawmill. Eight successive generations of Nyes lived in the house until in 1911 it was deeded to the commonwealth by Ray Nye. Subsequently the historic building was deeded to the Nye Family of America. Photograph courtesy of Rosanna Cullity

The Nickerson family reunion of September 1981. William Emery Nickerson arranged for the first reunion in June 1897 in Chatham. It has been held annually since except for a few years during World War I. Membership is open to anyone "bearing the name of Nickerson, any descendant of a Nickerson, or spouse of same." An annual newsletter keeps members in touch.

This family is representative of many with Cape roots who hold reunions, perpetuate traditions, preserve homesteads, and print genealogies. Photograph by Richard C. Kelsey; courtesy of the Nickerson Family Association, Inc.

The 1981 summer staff at the Craigville Conference Center. As in many resorts on the Cape, college students augment the year-round staff in summer months.

Left to right (from rear): Jackie Richardson, Craig White, Ann Washburn, Roger Washburn, Dexter Bliss, Jeff Tyner, Susan Parker, Dr. William F. Hobbs, (director), Steve Bush, Judy Perella, Edith Cahoon, Ruth Rodrick, David Tucker, Mark Tucker, Beth Parker, Cindy Quellhorst, Barbara Hobbs, Paul Hebert, Marcia Smith, Mindy Quellhorst, Charlie Liolios, and Erica Berry.

Not pictured: Margaret Cusick, Cindy Hobbs, Sharon Hobbs, Alison Hobbs, Kevin Overlock, Ellen Johnson, and Jo Ann Davis. Photograph by Kevin Schearer; courtesy of the Craigville Conference Center

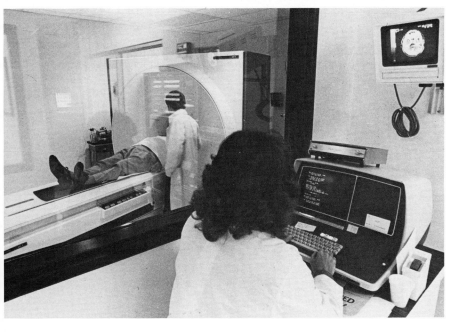

The CAT Scanner (Computerized Axial Tomography), added to the equipment of the Cape Cod Hospital in 1980, enables doctors to diagnose with extreme accuracy, thereby assuring more effective treatment. Photograph from Images; courtesy of Cape Cod Hospital

Medicenter Five, the newest of the medical facilities (1981), is a health care center providing year-round service to Brewster, Chatham, Eastham, Harwich, and Orleans residents. It gives basic medical care, health maintenance services, and minor emergency care not requiring the immediate care of a full service hospital. Drawing courtesy of Medicenter Five

"Marvelous" Marvin Hagler of Brockton, middleweight champion of the world, trained at the Provincetown Inn for his March fight in which he retained his title. Photograph by Stuart Eyman

The Dennis-Yarmouth Marching Band, participated in the Tournament of Roses parade in Pasadena, California, January 1, 1982. Photograph by Stuart Eyman

Young hockey players before a game in the Cape Cod Coliseum. Photograph by Dick Holbrook

Players from the Little Youth League of Yarmouth in a Memorial Day parade. Photograph by Dick Holbrook

Kerry Shank of Centerville urging Peck's Bad Boy over a jump at an English horse show. Photograph by Dick Holbrook

Debbie and David Clough of Osterville enjoy riding Western style along a trail. Photograph by Dick Holbrook

Cape Cod Times *editor William Breisky has a look at the paper's new computerized production system with staff member Gail Hennessey in March 1982. Photograph by Gordon E. Caldwell; courtesy of the* Cape Cod Times

FINE ARTS WORK CENTER

1981-82 VISUAL FELLOWS

The Visual Fellows of the 1981-82 Fine Arts Work Center in Provincetown enjoy a moment of relaxation.

In the late 1970s the center was established and since has provided more than 170 individuals with grants enabling them to continue or complete creative works. These include writing as well as visual fellows. Photograph courtesy of the Fine Arts Work Center

Just 362 years after the Pilgrims rounded the Cape tip in their fragile ship, an F-106 aircraft flies over it. United States Air Force planes, based at Otis Air National Guard Base, patrol regularly, guarding the land, the waters, and the people. Photograph courtesy of the Department of the Air Force, 102D Fighter Interceptor Wing, Massachusetts Air National Guard

BIBLIOGRAPHY

American People's Encyclopedia. Chicago: Spencer Press, 1948 plus continuing years.

Barber, John Warner. *Historical Collections of Every Town in Massachusetts.* Worcester, Dorr: Howland & Co., 1839.

Bradford, William. *History of Plymouth Plantation.* Boston: Wright & Potter, 1898.

Brand, Max. *Songs of '76.* New York: M. Evans & Co. Inc., 1972.

Brenizer, Meredith Marshall. *The Nantucket Indians.* Nantucket: Poet's Corner Press, 1976.

Burrows, Fredrika. *Yankee Scrimshanders.* Taunton: William S. Sullwold, Publishing, 1973.

Carpenter, Edmund J. *The Pilgrims and their Monument.* New York: D. Appleton & Co., 1911.

Deyo, Simeon L., *History of Barnstable County Massachusetts, 1620-1890.* New York: H. W. Blake, 1890.

Emerson, Amelia Forbes. *Early History of Naushon Island.* Boston: Trustees of Naushon Island Trust, Howland & Co., 1935.

Freeman, Frederick. *The History of Cape Cod: The Annals of Barnstable County and of its Several Towns, including the District of Mashpee.* Boston: Rand & Avery, 1862.

Fritz, Jean. *Cast For a Revolution.* Boston; Houghton Mifflin Co., 1972.

Geoffry, Theodate. *Saconnesset.* Falmouth, 1928.

Heavey, William F. *Down Ramp.* Washington: Infantry Journal, 1947.

Kittredge, Henry C. *Cape Cod: Its People and Their History.* Boston: Houghton Mifflin Co., 1968.

Lawson, Evelyn. *Theater on Cape Cod.* Yarmouth Port: Parnassus Imprints, 1969.

Lovell, Russell, Jr. *Notes on the History of the First Parish Church in Sandwich.* Sandwich: Bicentennial Commission, 1975.

McKenney, O. Herbert, and others. *The Seven Villages of Barnstable.* Town of Barnstable, 1976.

National Council of Congregational Churches in the United States. *Debts Hopeful and Desperate.* Boston: Pilgrim Press, 1963.

Perry, E. G. *A Trip Around Cape Cod.* Boston: Charles Binner & Co., 1898.

Peirce, Ebeneezer W. *Indian History, Biography and Genealogy, pertaining to the good sachem Massasoit of the Wampanoag tribe and his descendants.* North Abington: Zerviah Gould Mitchell, 1878.

Rich, Shebnah. *Truro Cape Cod.* Boston: D. Lothrop & Co., 1884.

Rinaldo, Karen. *Cape Cod/200.* Falmouth: Willard Weaner, 1976.

Starkloff, Carl. *The People of the Center: American Indian Religions and Christianity.* New York: Seabury Press, 1974.

Sears, Clara Endicot. *The Great Powwow.* Boston: Houghton Mifflin, 1934.

Trayser, Donald. *Barnstable: Three Centuries a Cape Cod Town.* Barnstable: F. B. and F. P. Goss, 1939.

Wood, Donald. *Cape Cod, A Guide.* Boston: Little Brown & Company, 1973.

Wood, William. *New England's Prospect.* Boston: Prince Society, 1865.

About the Author

Marion Vuilleumier is a feature writer for the magazines *Cape Cod People Today* and the *Cape Cod Compass*. She also reviews books for the *Cape Cod Times* and writes a column, "All About Books," for the Hughes Newspapers. In addition she edits the quarterly religious magazine *Transformation*. She has written fifteen books, some of which are: *Cape Cod in Color, Indians on Olde Cape Cod, Along the Wampanoag Trail, Sketches of Cape Cod, The Way It Was, Churches of Cape Cod, Boys and Girls on Olde Cape Cod, Martha's Vineyard in Color* and *Meditations By The Sea.*

As part of her community activities, Mrs. Vuilleumier is a member of the Barnstable Historical Commission, executive secretary of the Cape Cod Writers' Conference, and host of the weekly television show "Books and the World." She was recently elected a fellow of the Pilgrim Society in Plymouth and is a member of the Author's Guild, the National Book Critic's Circle, the National League of American Pen Women, as well as the local writing groups Twelve O'Clock Scholars and Professional Writers of Cape Cod. She teaches writing at the Cape Cod Community College.

Index

NAMES

A

Abdas 45
Agassiz, Louis 122
Aldrich, Richard 169, 180
Amos, Joseph "Blind Joe" 97
Andros, Edmund 30, 48
Atwood, Nat 110
Aumsequen 45
Avery, Edward 165

B

Bachiler, Stephen 34
Baker, Albert 151
Baker, Earl 139
Baker, Weston 89
Banks, Nathaniel 162
Baril, Robert F. 203
Barrows, Walter 172
Barry, Lawrence 163
Barzun, Jacques 192
Bates, Katharine Lee 142, 143
Baxter, Mrs. Sylvester 110
Bearse, Barbara 175
Bearse, Harry 139
Bearse, Jean McKenzie 175
Bearse, Nelson 165
Bearse, Thurlow 139
Bellamy, Samuel 63
Belmont, August 154, 156, 162
Benedict, Ely 149
Benn, John 209
Berry, Erica 215
Beston, Henry 173, 210
Blaney, George 197
Bleiken, John 175
Bliss, Dexter 215
Boardley, Benjamin F. 145
Boardman, Russell 184
Bolles, Carl 173
Boody, L. M. 125
Borden, John 36
Bourne, Benjamin 58
Bourne, Richard 35, 46
Bourne, Silas 77
Bourne, Sylvanus 60
Bourne, Timothy 60
Bradford, Ernest 139
Bradford, Myron 139
Bradford, Stuart 165
Bradford, William 27, 34, 39, 162
Bray, Mrs. Thomas 105
Breisky, William 218
Brewster, William 22
Brice, John 131
Britton, Scott 203
Brooke, Edward 200
Browne, Thelma Johnson 175
Browne, John 45
Buffington, James 200
Bunting, Keith 197
Burgess, S. C. 147
Burgess, Thornton W. 123, 143, 178
Bush, Steve 215

C

Cahoon, Bill 131
Cahoon, Edith 215
Carlson, Mary 71
Cash, Alexander 139
Casper, Richard 213
Cataldo, Louis 71, 72, 188, 197
Cataloni, Joseph 203
Challies, Michael 203
Chamberlain, Ralph 186
Chamberlayne, Nathan Henry 98
Champlain, Samuel de 14, 15
Chase, H. B. 136
Chase, Henry E. 19
Chase, Lafayette 141
Chase, Lewis Arthur 45
Chase, William 38
Chipman, Isaac 93
Chipman, Melinda Nye Fish 93
Clagg, Charles 186

Clarke, Valerie 199
Claybrook, Robert 102
Cleveland, Stephen Grover 117, 123, 132, 14
Clough, David 217
Clough, Debbie 217
Colby, Roy 199
Colby, Ruth 199
Columbo, Lou 213
Coombs, Mrs. Elizabeth 173
Cotton, John 46
Covell, William 197
Crane, Mrs. Alexander 82
Crocker, Alfred 115, 141, 147
Crocker, Harriet 129
Crocker, John 56
Crocker, John Howland 175
Crocker, Kathleen 147
Crocker, Lauchlan 179
Crocker, Loring 59
Crocker, Ruth 147, 153
Crump, William 150
Crump, William, Jr. 150
Cusick, Martha 215
Cutchamakin 45

D

DaLuz, Joseph 204
Davis, Henry 186
Davis, Jo Ann 215
Davis, Thomas 63
Dennis, Josiah 34, 56
De Rasieres, Isaac 30
Dickens, Minica 192, 210
Dickenson, Edwin 213
Dimmock, Joseph 58, 67
Doane, George, W. 136
Donaldson, Sylvia 173
Downs, Isaac 89
Draper, Eben S. 153
Dwight, Timothy 49

E

Eaton, Theoph 45
Edwards, Clarence 163, 182
Edwards, Mrs. Martha 173
Edwards, Selina 173
Eliot, John 35, 44, 45, 46
Elliott, Robert 165
Enow, Maureen 213

F

Fenwick, George 45
Ferguson, Hugh 168
Flinkman Dagmar 175
Flint, Sadie F. 133
Fowell, Myron 200
Freeman, Abigail 64
Freeman, Clarendon 141
Freeman, Edmund 34
Freeman, Nathaniel 141
Fuller, Stephen 175

G

Gardner, Mrs. Dorcas 173
Gardner, Elizabeth 175
Gardner, Frances 175
Genander, Larry 160
Gifford, Charles L. 186
Gifford, Franklin Lewis 67, 78
Gill, Geraldine 201
Goodyeare, Steven 45
Gosnold, Bartholomew 14, 16
Grant, Ulysses S. 123
Greim, Christopher 203
Guild, Curtis, Jr. 151

H

Hackett, Bobby 213
Hagler, Marvin 216
Hall, Christopher 84
Hall, Henry 83
Hallett, Clara Jane 188
Hallett, Dudley 214
Hallett, Elmer 131
Hallett, Josiah H. 84
Hallett, N. T. 131

Hamlin, Deborah 105
Hamlin, Joseph Eldridge 104, 105
Hamlin, Micah 67
Harding, Samuel 63
Harrington, Patricia 71
Harris, Agnes 204
Harris, Leighton 204
Harrison, Benjamin 54
Harrison, George 54
Hartford, Nathaniel Bourne 29
Hatch, Abigail Swift 99
Hatch, Barnabas 99
Hatch, Isaiah 99
Hawthorne, Charles W. 208
Hennessey, Gail 218
Herbert, Jeanne 209
Hergesheimer, Heidi 203
Hewins, William 79
Hinckley, Oliver 99
Hinckley, Thomas 36, 48
Hinckley, Woodrow 99
Hobbs, Alison 215
Hobbs, Barbara 215
Hobbs, Cindy 215
Hobbs, Sharon 215
Hobbs, William 215
Holmes, William 91
Holway, John A. 141
Hopkins, Edward 45
Howes, William Frederick 84
Howland, Alfred 131
Hughes, John 211
Hughes, Libby 211
Hutchinson, Thomas 105

J

Jaques, Paul 204
Jarves, Deming 82, 104
Jeffers, Lorenzo (Chief Mittark) 200
Jefferson, Joseph 117, 118
Jefferson, Thomas 59
Johnson, Ellen 215
Johnson, Evelyn 199
Johnson, Harry 175
Johnson, Oscar 89, 175
Johnson, Paul 199
Jones, Charles Carroll 140, 141
Jones, Thomas Warren 106
Julian, John 63

K

Keith, Eben 95
Keith, Isaac 82, 94, 95
Keith, Edward, Jr. 95
Kelley, F. G. 114
Kennedy, Carolyn 193
Kennedy, Edward 204, 214
Kennedy, Jacqueline (see Onassis) 193
Kennedy, John Fitzgerald 190, 193-96
Kennedy, John Fitzgerald, Jr. 196
Kennedy, Joseph 184, 193-95
Kennedy, Joseph, Jr. 184
Kennedy, Robert 193-95
Kennedy, Rose 193
Kenney, James F. 185
Kenny, Nathan 43
King, Edward 204, 214

L

Lane, Merle 175
Lavalle, Gregory 203
Lawes, Virginia 185
Lawrence, Gertrude 169, 180, 186
Lawrence, Harry Vincent 134
Lawrence, Mary Chipman 86
Lawrence, Samuel 86
Lenart, Stephen 203
Lewis, Harry 172
Lincoln, Abraham 104, 105
Lincoln, Freeman 142
Lincoln, Joseph Crosby 123, 142
Lioliost, Charles 215
Littlefield, Ruth Lovequist 175
Lodge, Henry Cabot 151
Lombard, Percival Hale 29
Lothrop, Freeman L. 141

Lothrop, John 34, 41
Lovell, George 104
Lovequist, Lawrence 175

M

Madison, James 77
Maher, Roy 165
Maki, Frank Jr. 72
Marconi, Guglielmo 69, 123
Marcus, Marie 213
Massasoit 22, 26, 36, 200
McNaughton, Joan Allen 174
McKenna, Dave 213
Melville, Herman 86
Memmolo, Dante 209
Messer, Augustus 146
Meekasano 45
Mittark (Lorenzo Jeffers) 200
Moore, Edward 203
Moran, Brian 203
Mosley, Emerson 204
Mosley, Margaret 204
Munson, Thurmon 184
Murphy, Thomas 197, 200
Murray, Betty 203
Murray, Robert J. 203
Murray, Victoria Ann 203

N

Nash, Royston 213
Nelson, Elna Ruska 175
Nightingale, Lloyd 77
Nickerson, Allen 141
Nickerson, Violet Siira 175
Nickerson, William Brewster 201
Nickerson, William Emery 215
Noon, Philo G. 175
Nute, Fred 165
Nye, Benjamin 214
Nye, Ray 214
Nye, William 9

O

O'Brien, Mary 209
Olney, Richard 132
Onassis, Jacqueline Kennedy 193
O'Neill, Eugene 169
Otis, Frank 182
Otis, James 58
Otis, James, Jr. 57, 64
Otis, John 60
Otis, Joseph 58, 67
Overlock, Kevin 215

P

Palches, Lois 198, 199
Palches, Peter 197-99
Park, Douglas 203
Parker, Beth 215
Parker, Susan 215
Parker, Thomas 162
Parker, Ward 78
Peirce, Ebeneezer W. 26
Peirce, Palo Alto 26
Pell, David 203
Pells, Priscilla 173
Penniman, Augusta 133
Penniman, Edward 133
Percival, Henry 141
Percival, John "Mad Jack" 76
Perella, Judy 215
Perry, Elsa 165
Pessecouss 45
Peters, Charles 173
Peterson, Penny 203
Philbrook, Richard 203
Philip (Pometecom or Metecomet) 36
Phillips, Gladys 175
Piercy, Marge 192
Pocknett, Anna 173
Pocknett, Mrs. Sarah 173
Polando, John 184
Pometecom (Philip or Metacomet) 36
Pooke, Samuel · 84
Prence, Thomas (Prince) 43, 45, 46
Price, Charlotte 201, 214

Pring, Martin 14
Pummash 45

Q

Quachatisset 35
Quadequina 22
Quellhorst, Mindy 215
Quippish, Eben 17

R

Raggot, Richard 59, 77
Reed, Gladys 203
Rhodes, Frank 204
Richards, Eleanor 185
Richards, Elmer, A. E. 185
Richardson, Jackie 215
Ricketts, Kathleen 203
Rinaldo, Karen 68
Robichau, Candace 203
Robinson, John 23
Robinson, Lydia 98
Roderick, Ruth 215
Roosevelt, Theodore 123, 151-53
Rudman, Gloria 72
Ruska, William 175
Russell, Jonathan 59
Ryder, Carlton 131
Ryder, Harry 131
Ryder, John L. 105

S

Salo, Henry 19
Sanna, John 203

Scallon, Dorthy 175
Schilling, Mary 199
Schley, Eleanor 209
Scruggs, Roseann 203
Sears, J. Henry 151, 153
Sears, John 83
Semprini, Betty Hazelton 175
Shank, Kerry 217
Shaw, Bill 133
Shaw, Lemuel 97
Shirley, William 60
Siira, Barbara 175
Simons, Nelson 173
Simons, William 173
Small, Charles 203
Small, Isaac 75
Smith, Frances 133, 135
Smith, John 14, 18
Smith, Marcia 215
Smith, Sarah 133
Snider, Mark 214
Snow, Henry 179
Soller, Barbara 53
Soller, William 53
Soule, Thomas 141
Southworth, Thomas 46
Sprague, Mary 48
Squanto 26, 27
Stallknecht, Alice 189
Standish, Myles 34, 84
Starck, Carl 165
Starck, Elsa 175
Starck, Inga 175

Starck, Russell 165, 175
Stevens, Carroll 165
Stratton, Roy 210
Sturgis, William 41
Swift, Charles 131
Swift, Elijah 78
Swift, Mrs. Frances 133, 135
Swift, Gustavus Franklin 117
Swift, Thomas 78

T

Taft, William Howard 123, 153
Thacher, Anthony 34
Thacher, John 48
Theroux, Paul 192
Thompson, Charles 141
Thoreau, Henry David 123
Totten, Ella Stephenson 89
Treat, Samuel 35
Tucker, David 215
Tucker, Mark 215
Tyner, Jeff 215

V

Valkenier, Willem 213
Vincent, Herbert 131
Vivante, Arturo 209
Vonnegut, Kurt, Jr. 192, 210
Vuilleumier, Louis 210
Vuilleumier, Marion 71, 211
Vuilleumier, Pierre DuPont 200

W

Walker, Robert 27
Walsh, George 84
Wamsutta 36
Ward, Jean 209
Warner, John 71
Warren, Bert 133
Warren, James 59
Warren, Mercy Otis 59, 65
Washburn, Ann 215
Washburn, Roger 215
Washburn, Ruth 98
Webster, Daniel 82, 97
Weigert, Agnes 175
Weigert, Barry 175
Weston, Hercules 91
White, Alvin 213
White, Craig 215
White, Ernest 213
White, Mildred Cole 175
Whitfield, George 57
Williams, Stephen 72
Wilson, Harold, Jr. 210
Winslow, Edward 22, 27
Winthrop, James 162
Winthrop, John 34, 45
Witham, Barbara 210
Witowash 45
Wood, William 31
Woolley, Catherine 202
Worrell, Dorothy 188, 197
Worrell, Elisha 179
Wright, William 54
Wueppish, Eben 173

SUBJECTS

A

Angle Tree Stone 38
Aptucxet Trading Post 22, 28, 29, 30, 53, 149
Association for the Preservation of Cape Cod 194
Atwood House 56

B

Baptist 44, 57, 66, 97
Barnstable County 36
Barnstable County Agricultural
  Society 116, 118, 169
Barnstable Town 10, 34, 40, 41, 44, 48, 53, 56,
  59, 68, 73, 82, 90, 105, 174, 175, 178, 179
Barnstable, England 34, 179
Bicentennial, National 66, 68-72
Billingsgate 84
Boston and Sandwich Glass Co. 54, 82, 93,
  110, 210
Bourne, Town 14, 28, 34, 44, 53, 98, 102, 82
  149, 156, 165, 172
Bournedale 47
Bournehurst-on-the-Canal 172
Brewster, Town 44, 56, 69, 96, 101, 105, 123,
  130, 132, 135, 140, 203, 216
Brugessm Thornton W. Society 210
Buzzards Bay 105, 122, 170, 203, 214

C

Cape Cod Art Association 184, 209
Cape Cod Canal 154-162
Cape Cod Chamber of Commerce 168, 183
Cape Cod Coliseum 192, 216
Cape Cod Community College 184, 201
Cape Cod Community Council 192
Cape Cod Conservatory of Music
  and Arts 184, 211, 212, 213
Cape Cod Council of Churches 99, 192
Cape Cod Hospital 168, 192, 208, 215
Cape Cod Museum of Natural History 194
Cape Cod National Seashore Park 19, 193
Cape Cod Planning and Economic Development
  Commission 194
Cape Cod Symphony Orchestra 184, 213
Cape Cod Writers' Conference 192, 202, 209
Centerville 114, 120, 124, 179
Chatham 35, 44, 56, 58, 73, 75, 82, 96, 100,
  111, 186, 164, 202, 203, 216
Christian Camp Meeting Association 122, 131,
  148, 200
Christiantown 44
Churches 32, 37, 41, 44, 53, 57, 66, 69, 89, 106,
  133, 156, 168, 173, 175, 182, 186, 189, 192, 199
Cotuit 110, 122, 186

Courthouse 58, 66, 163
Craigville 120, 122, 131, 200, 215
Cranberry 83, 90, 91, 110
Customs Houses 72, 73
Cuttyhunk 16

D

Dennis, Town 34, 44, 56, 73, 82, 83, 84, 198
  203, 216
Dexter Mill 56
Dillingham House 56

E

Eastham 44, 52, 56, 89, 119, 135, 173,
  203, 216
Edwards, Camp 163, 182, 187
Elder Services of Cape Cod and the
  Islands 192, 214

F

Falmouth 34, 44, 53, 56, 58, 60, 67, 68, 73,
  77, 88, 97, 104, 110, 115, 122, 124, 126, 132
  133, 134, 156, 173, 201, 203, 209, 214
Falmouth Artists' Guild 209
Falmouth Hospital 193, 197
Falmouth National Bank 78, 201
Fine Arts Work Center 218
French Cable Station 123, 127
Food 14, 15, 27, 28, 53, 83, 168, 194, 204, 214

G

Glauber Salt 90
Grace, Doreen Center 205
Gray Gables 123, 149, 150
Gypsies 115

H

Harwich 44, 67, 82, 203, 216
Heritage Plantation 62, 200
Highland Light 75, 82
Hoxie House 39, 53, 56, 90
Hyannis 73, 110, 115, 122, 124, 128, 136, 137
  156, 163, 182, 186, 198, 201, 203
Hyannis Port 122, 125, 156, 172

I

Indians 12-19, 22, 26, 28, 30, 35, 36, 39,
  44-7, 63, 174
Inns (ordinaries) 49, 56, 57
Iron works 83, 91

K

Keith Manufacturing Company 82, 83, 94
Kennedy Memorial 69, 198
King Philip's War 36, 44, 47

L

Liberty Cap 70
Liberty Hall 89, 110
Liberty Pole 58, 66
Libraries 110, 201, 214
Life Saving Service 82, 111-13
Lighthouses 73, 75, 82, 108, 110
Lyceums 142

M

Marine Biological Laboratory 205
Martha's Vineyard 14, 36, 44, 98, 182, 203
Mashpee (Marshpee) 16, 17, 35, 36, 44, 46, 57,
  69, 173, 183, 205
Massachusetts Bay Colony 30, 34, 37
Massachusetts Maritime Academy 122
Mayflower Compact 22, 23
Medicenter Five 193, 216
Militia, Barnstable County 58, 70, 77
Militia, Falmouth 58, 70
Mills 34, 50, 51, 52, 54, 56, 60, 62
Monument Beach 48, 114, 148

N

Nantucket 82, 182
Nauset 15, 19, 35, 123
Naushon 16, 76
New Alchemy Institute 194
New Amsterdam 22, 30
New Seabury 183, 205
Newspapers 60, 183, 218
Nickerson Family of America 215
Nobska Lighthouse 108, 110
Nye, E. B. Post No. 203 105
Nye Homestead 56, 214

O

Old Colony Club 144
Old Colony Railroad 85
Orleans 44, 59, 62, 77, 96, 123, 127, 203, 216
Osterville 122, 124, 199
Otis Air Force Base 111
Otis Air National Guard Base 219
Outermost House 173, 210
Oyster Harbors 178

P

Pacific Guano Company 114
Packet boats 56, 82
Pairpoint Glass Company 210
Parker Mills 83
Patriots 58, 64
Penikese Island 122
Penzance Point 114
Pilgrim Memorial Monument 23, 68, 151, 153

Pilgrims 20-31
Plimoth Plantation 22, 25, 26, 30, 34, 37, 38
Plymouth County 36
Plymouth (Plimoth) 20-31, 37, 38, 45, 52
Pocasset Iron Company 91, 92
Pope House 56
Population 57, 82, 110, 168, 192
Powder House 67
Provincetown 14, 22, 23, 44, 49, 60, 68, 82, 96, 111, 182, 186, 208, 216, 218
Puritans 34, 38

Q
Quakers (Society of Friends) 34, 57

R
Radio 183
Railroad 79, 83, 85, 95, 96, 145, 146, 183, 214

S
Saconesset Homestead 56
Sacrament Rock 34, 40
Sagamore 159, 210
Salt works 59, 77, 83, 90

Sandwich 34, 37, 40, 44, 53, 54, 56-8, 69, 73, 82, 90, 93, 98, 104, 110, 178, 203
Santuit 110
Schools 90, 119, 122, 124, 125, 129, 164, 174, 175, 184, 216
Scrooby Club 175
Ships 20, 22, 35, 38, 43, 59, 76-8, 81, 82, 84, 85-7, 130, 143, 149, 152, 161, 182, 187, 203
Shiverick Shipyards 82, 84
Sixty-fourth Regiment of Foot 77
Skiffe House 56
Sports 12, 85, 91, 115, 116, 129, 130, 132, 165, 172, 174, 184, 192, 217
Stage coaches 56, 57, 79

T
Tales of Cape Cod 58, 66, 188, 197
Tarpaulin Cove 58, 59, 76
Telephone 127, 128
Television 183, 184, 211
Theater 169, 176, 202
Tories (Loyalists) 58, 64
Trolley cars 148
Truro 44, 52, 56, 100, 202

U
United Colonies of New England 45
United States Coast Guard 73

V
Vikings 14
Volunteers of Cape Cod 193

W
Wampanoags (see also Indians) 12-19, 35, 44
Wampanoag Indian Museum 16, 17
Wampum 30
Waquoit 200
Wareham 83, 203
Whaling 56, 82, 86, 87, 88, 91, 198
Wianno 122
Wing Family of America 39, 40, 144
Wing Fort House 39, 144
Woods Hole 73, 110, 111, 114, 122, 204, 205

Y
Yarmouth Brass Band 131
Yarmouth Camp Ground Association 89
Yarmouth, Town 32, 34, 42, 44, 49, 53, 56, 74, 89, 90, 110, 124, 131, 177, 192, 203, 210, 216, 217